Finding my voice

Finding my voice

RACHEL STEVENS

A STORY OF STRENGTH, SELF-BELIEF AND S CLUB

HarperCollins*Publishers*

HarperCollins*Publishers*
1 London Bridge Street
London SE1 9GF

www.harpercollins.co.uk

HarperCollins*Publishers*
Macken House, 39/40 Mayor Street Upper
Dublin 1, D01 C9W8, Ireland

First published by HarperCollins*Publishers* 2024

1 3 5 7 9 10 8 6 4 2

A catalogue record of this book is
available from the British Library

ISBN 978-0-00-866217-2

Printed and bound in the UK using 100%
renewable electricity at CPI Group (UK) Ltd

This book contains FSC™ certified paper and other controlled
sources to ensure responsible forest management.

For more information visit: www.harpercollins.co.uk/green

CONTENTS

Chapter 24
FINDING ME

PROLOGUE

IT WAS 27 FEBRUARY 2024, the final show of the S Club *Good Times* tour in the US. Walking off stage at the Orpheum Theatre in Los Angeles, I felt completely overwhelmed. The tour had been a mix of ups, downs and everything in between. On that last night, knowing it was the final show, I came off stage full of so many emotions, I didn't feel quite ready for all the post-show celebrations.

LA was the perfect place to end our tour, a home from home with so many memories. The show was so full of joy, and the buzz and love in the room were beautiful. While there were times where I was at my most confident, there were others where I felt vulnerable. As always, this came from putting myself out there and feeling exposed, hearing the same old voices telling me to pull it back and not to be too … too what?

After this last show, however, as overwhelmed as I was, I had a moment of clarity, realising how far I'd come and where I was going. Backstage, I could hear everyone in the halls celebrating, and at first, I wanted to lock myself away in my dressing room. Instead, I took a breath and listened to my voice telling me exactly what I needed. It was the simple act of giving myself a moment, the space to breathe.

Once my friends left, I just felt like I needed to ground myself. I lay down on the floor, still and quiet, to connect to what I was feeling instead of judging or ignoring it. From that moment came a release of emotions simply because I'd allowed myself to feel. For once, I had not buried my wants, needs and feelings and pushed them away, which is pretty much what I'd done my whole life.

It feels freeing and empowering to know I'm on the right path to hearing, trusting and finding my voice.

Chapter 1

ON THE SURFACE

APPEARANCES, AND HOW things looked on the outside, counted for a lot in my family. In many ways, I grew up feeling quite image-conscious. It was ingrained in me from a very young age, I felt, the importance of how others saw me and saw us as a family. It became the principal thing I had to hold on to over the years. What was on the surface became my armour.

As I got older, and throughout my career, looking good became even more of a focus, and a thread throughout my life. For a while, it felt good having people talk about my appearance, especially when it was generally in positive terms. At times, I craved it; I measured my worth against how I looked, how others perceived me and how I felt I should be. Our image and the way we look is just a part of who we are, but over time, so much of me became that. The truth is, if what's inside goes unnurtured, you can end up wondering who you really are.

As time went on, I found myself asking questions about why I was struggling with anxiety, relationships, and why I often felt sad and uneasy. I realised I needed to change all that and search for much more. I had to look hard and dig deep because I'd spent so long repressing it, scared of what I might find … or not find.

Author and politician Marianne Williamson once wrote, 'Our deepest fear is not that we are inadequate. Our deepest fear is that we are powerful beyond measure.'*

This quote really resonates with me. For so long, there was so much inside me that I couldn't find the words or voice to express. I never knew how my true voice might sound or even who I was. Many of the things I thought or believed to be true as a child had, over time, been turned into mistrust, lies, deceit and betrayal, which left me feeling like I couldn't even trust myself.

Thankfully, my determination to grow pushed me through, and eventually I started to ask myself questions. The voice in my head telling me that there had to be more got louder and clearer. I've always known the value of pushing myself out of my comfort zone, and striving to be the best version of myself has been one of my great passions – a driving force deep within me. These are the things that have got me to where I am now, and I'm grateful to have this opportunity to share my story.

It's taken a long time, been a slow process and, of course, I sometimes still feel the triggers of the past and experience

* Marianne Williamson, *A Return to Love: Reflections on the Principles of 'A Course in Miracles'* (1992)

feelings of wanting to hide away in my shell. Ultimately, I'm still working on myself, as we always are, but am so thankful to be on the journey of self-discovery that I am on and for life's adventures.

I was the middle child, born between two brothers in the spring of 1978. 'Night Fever' by the Bee Gees was number one in the charts, and my mum tells me the ground was thick with snow on the day I was born.

My parents had met on the West End club circuit in the early Seventies, at a club called Tiffany's. Mum recalls the first night they met, Dad circling the dance floor with his eye on her. She grew up in Staines, and my dad in Ilford, East London, and although she was five years younger, Dad says he was struck by her beauty. It was about a year after that first meeting that he called her out of the blue, asking her to be his date at a party he'd been invited to. She agreed, and the two of them met at the Cumberland Hotel, near Marble Arch, then headed off to the party together. When Dad dropped her home in Staines that night, he made a cheeky joke about needing a passport to get there, with it being so far outside London. He was charming and charismatic from the off, in fact my grandma Pearl – my mum's mother – couldn't quite believe what she was seeing when they met.

'There must be something wrong with him,' she told Mum. 'He's too good to be true.'

Of course, Dad had given Grandma the works – he was dressed immaculately, incredibly polite and even stood every time she did. He was always wonderful at that, my dad, turning on the charm! From everything that I've heard, Grandma Pearl was as bowled over as Mum, who was just as smitten with Dad as he was with her.

My older brother, Jason, came nearly four years before me, and then Leigh – a happy surprise – eighteen months after. I sometimes wonder if having two brothers so close in age was one of the reasons I could be more comfortable in the company of boys than girls as a child. It's not surprising, I suppose; ours was a boy-heavy family. As well as my brothers, all my cousins were boys, too. Consequently, as well as playing with dolls, I also grew up watching *Rambo*, and playing with Micro Machines. Surely most kids in the Eighties watched at least one of the *Rocky* movies? I watched all of them.

My brothers and I got on well most of the time – although they were typical brothers. We sometimes fought, as most siblings do, to the point where once I actually called the police on them. And they would do the usual horrible brother stuff – scaring me, locking me in the bathroom (I have no idea why we had a lock on the outside of our bathroom, but we did) or smothering me under the bed covers until I couldn't breathe.

Other than that, we weren't all that naughty as children. My dad was sometimes quite hot-tempered, so we rarely even swore, but if we ever did, we'd know about it. Once,

Dad chased me up the stairs for swearing, and just managed to catch me on the leg with his hand – and wow, did it sting! I had a red handprint to remind me to mind my Ps and Qs. Mum, on the other hand, never really lost her temper – at least, I don't remember her doing so. In many ways, I felt that my mum was quite passive, and for the most part would have done anything to keep the peace (as a parent, I can relate to that). Mum was the one who ran the house, day-to-day, making sure we had everything we needed. She was a hairdresser by profession, and she always worked, apart from when we were all very young. My dad's profession is harder to put my finger on. He was a salesman, of sorts, but his work varied and I was never quite sure exactly what it was. Honestly, I don't have enough chapters in the book to share his colourful working history, but oh, is it colourful!

Although I loved clothes, make-up and experimenting with every beauty product my mum owned, I also loved getting stuck in with what we thought of as stereotypical boys' stuff – and tearing around the streets on wheels. Friends of my parents had a roller-skate shop, so when roller skates were a big thing, we had the best ones. My brothers also had bikes called Raleigh Vektars, which were the first ever computerised bike.

We did that a lot back then, playing outside in the street. Much more so than children do now, I think. We'd often be out until ten at night, playing on our bikes with all the other kids on our street. We always felt quite safe though, or maybe we just didn't even think about it. We just loved being outside. Playing out was fun and exciting. There were certain smells and sounds to it – trees and cut grass, distant traffic and planes flying overhead. It was freedom and adventure.

I sometimes wonder if our parents had it easier in those days, when kids were content with simpler things like running around outside and inventing their own games and amusement. In the high-tech, fast-paced twenty-first century, parenting feels much more intense. Back in the Eighties, we'd be out in the fresh air, out of our parents' hair, and there didn't seem to be any worries about it.

Growing up, my dad, brothers and I loved cars – particularly classic cars. The one that stands out most from my childhood was a Trans Am, exactly like the one in the American TV show *Knight Rider*. It was white and had a red leather interior – very Eighties. Add to that Mum's very big hair and even bigger shoulder pads – think Krystle Carrington from *Dynasty* – and we're talking a strong retro aesthetic!

I remember the looks I'd get when Dad would drop me at school in the Trans Am, and some of the boys getting excited seeing the car. You could always hear us coming a mile off with the roar of the engine.

Back then, I loved watching TV shows like *Knight Rider*, *Street Hawk*, *The A-Team* and other classics with my brothers. It's funny how kids of today won't know the urgency of doing anything you needed to do during the ad breaks of a TV show, so you didn't miss a second of your favourite programme.

There was also a fantastic selection of board games back then, with classics like Operation, Battleships, Guess Who?, Marble Run, and not forgetting Pac-Man! I enjoyed playing games with my friends and with my brothers, and I was always very competitive. Connect4 was a favourite of mine, as well as Hotel, which was a game where you built hotels and resorts on the board while trying to drive your fellow players into bankruptcy.

All that said, I was always, and still am, a girl's girl. Yet I was sometimes intimidated by them. I never felt like I quite fitted in, or that I was 'one of the girls'. Looking back, I realise that one of the reasons for that was because, from a young age, I was missing a sense of an emotional connection with some of the influential women in my life.

As a child, subconsciously, I had a sense of fitting in to a mould that suited others, even when it didn't feel right to me. *Don't voice an opinion. Look pretty. Be nice. She's shy!* The list goes on and on. As the mum of two girls now, I do my best not to label them – or anyone else for that matter. Aren't we all a bit of everything – complex and perfectly imperfect? But that word – perfect – was always something I thought I had to strive to be. To this day, I'm still fighting that need for perfectionism, although much less now as I know there is no such thing, and learning where my boundaries are.

Our house was on a little cul-de-sac in Southgate, North London. It didn't have a lot of character as buildings go, just a three-bed semi, which Mum and Dad made more than the best of. While the outside may not have been remarkable, the interior was quite grand. In many ways, it was like a show home – always perfect, always pristine. Mum was very house-proud, and still is. We had a smart front door, plush carpets, stylish furniture and a lot of nice things, all perfectly placed. As we got older, my parents made improvements and built an extension, as many people did, which meant my brothers could have separate rooms. My younger brother's new room in the extension had all those classic Eighties touches – graphic black, white and red print wallpaper and a stereo system. My bedroom was mint green and, just like in the rest of the house, everything had to have its place. I was firm about that. At one point, if anyone sat on my bed I had to smooth it all out as soon as they left; I wonder if that was the start of a need to control and have order in my life. My room was always immaculately tidy – lucky mum. As I got a bit older, I had my own TV. Getting my first stereo was also something special; I was so excited at the idea that I could listen to music in my room. I had quite the cassette collection, and there was a lot of singing into my hairbrush pretending to be a popstar. Madonna was an early favourite, as were George Michael, Kylie Minogue,

Rick Astley and Jason Donovan. I wouldn't say we were spoilt, but we certainly never went without as kids, not when it came to having stuff.

As a Jewish family, we weren't particularly religious, although my maternal grandparents, Pearl, whom we lovingly referred to as 'Pearl Jam', and grandpa Alan, both observed many of the Jewish high holy days. My parents, less so. As kids, we always observed Rosh Hashanah – Jewish New Year – and Yom Kippur – the holiest day on the Jewish calendar – but we would always be the family that drove to Shul and ducked down so nobody could see us. On Jewish holy days, you're not supposed to drive, but we always did. To be honest, the synagogue was too far from our house to walk, so if we hadn't driven, we'd have probably not got there at all. We had Friday-night dinner, though there was never really any structure involved – it was as and when. But what I've taken from being Jewish is the idea of family being together, community and some of the traditions.

That said, one of my fondest memories growing up was around Passover. On the first two nights you welcome in the holy day, usually with family and friends, saying an order of prayers and traditions. One of these was hiding some matzah (flatbread) around the house, and then whoever found it won a reward. I'd run around with my cousins frantically searching everywhere. It was always a happy

family moment, and one of the many lovely memories I
have of us all being together at my grandma's house in
Staines. I always felt a warm comfort there. Something
about being surrounded by my whole family made me feel
safe and secure. On top of that, my grandparents lived close
to Heathrow Airport. It was always so exciting for us as
kids, looking out of the window as the planes roared over
our heads when they took off or came in to land.

When I was five, I went to a little private school along
with my older brother. I was only there for a couple of terms,
but then my parents couldn't afford to keep us there, so I
moved to a state primary school called Osidge, which was
just opposite. I stayed there for the rest of my primary years.

I found school difficult at times. I never really felt like I
fitted in; I certainly wasn't part of any in-crowd or the
popular group – and that stayed the same all the way
through. In fact, right through primary school, I experienced a lot of unkindness, which was upsetting, and because
it happened so often, I felt like I was being bullied. It wasn't
the head-flushed-down-the-toilet kind of bullying; it was
more general nastiness, bitchiness and being pushed around.
I don't know why I was singled out for it; I guess nobody
does when they're a young child. I just knew how much it
hurt, and I came home from school most days very upset.
The problem built over time, with one particular girl being
the ringleader. After she hit me in the face and gave me a
nosebleed, Dad went round to her house to speak to her

parents. I'm not sure it did any good. It's funny, I can still remember her house; in fact, I drove past it just the other day, wondering what she might be doing now.

I remember my mum and dad telling me at the time, 'Oh, they're just jealous.'

Jealous of what? I always wondered. I had no clue why someone might envy me. The only thing I knew was that I didn't feel like I was part of any group, gang or circle. I was an outsider, although I'm not sure I'd have put it into those words as a child. I just felt different.

I know Mum and Dad were just trying to help and make me feel better, but now, as a parent myself, I know that what I really needed them to say was, 'I'm sorry you're going through this, it must be really horrible.' I guess what I'm trying to say here is that I don't feel like my feelings were ever validated as a child. This is not a 'poor me' moment; as a parent I understand how hard it is when your kids are struggling. I've learned through experience that children need to feel heard and seen, and it didn't feel like that was the case for me.

My secondary school, Ashmole, was massive, and I got lost in it. It wasn't that I wasn't academic – we all learn differently – I was just never inspired by my teachers. I felt like I was just a number and got a bit lost in the whole system. My school reports would say things like, *'If Rachel stopped talking in class, she'd improve greatly.'* They were right, I *was* a talker, given the opportunity; probably bored with the lessons and chatting to one of the boys, or whoever was sitting next to me. That said, I'd like to write reports for some of those teachers stating that if they'd been more engaging and exciting, perhaps I wouldn't have talked so much.

In secondary school, I feel like there was a lack of care around what my strengths might or might not be. It's funny, I don't remember any adult playing a big part in my education or personal growth, or even anyone showing much interest. Of course, there were teachers who taught, but throughout school there wasn't much in the way of guidance or nurturing. Nobody ever asked, 'What do you want to do, Rachel?'

Even at home, my parents didn't push me much or show strong interest in my education or after-school activities. I'm not sure they saw school as particularly important – it was just something we did daily. There wasn't really any structure for us to do our homework, or any thoughts of making sure we were studying or revising when we needed to.

I cared, though – so much. I wanted to do well. Inside, I was very driven, but I felt uninspired. My real drive came from the thought of getting out into the world, to live life and to start earning money. I had so much passion in me, but no one to advise me or nurture it.

It didn't help that the girls who'd given me a hard time at primary school also went to Ashmole, so the bullying continued. I was a bit of a loner, someone who didn't really have friends, because I didn't know who I could trust. Sadly this was sometimes the case with my friends outside school too. Lots of people I know have friends who they've known since their school days, which is lovely, but that wasn't the case for me. My friendships were built out-of-school and I'm grateful for them all.

My feelings of mistrust started early on. It was a mixture of things that stopped me letting people in. At home there were emotional walls building. I grew up in a house where we didn't really talk about anything. We didn't discuss our feelings or emotions, and, as children, we weren't really asked our opinions. It was very much a 'children are seen but not heard' situation. When we were kids, the adults around us never explained or discussed anything with us. Things would happen, and people would come into our lives and disappear without explanation. My uncle's wife, for instance. She was someone I was close to in some ways. She was that cool auntie many of us have; the one who helped me pick out clothes and do my make-up. As a mother of three boys, she may perhaps have seen me a bit like the daughter she never had. She took me to get my ears pierced, and bought me perfume and make-up. After she and my uncle (Mum's brother) got divorced, when I was ten or eleven, I never saw her again. No explanation, no gentle let-down. She was just gone. I never asked questions about what had happened to her because we didn't grow up in the kind of environment where that seemed an option. We just accepted what was in front of us and carried on.

As I said, we never wanted for anything, and we were always looked after and cared for, but real emotional connection was missing in our house, although there was a lot of laughter and love. There weren't many family dinners growing up, which I would have loved. I wonder if it's something of a generational thing. In fact, we didn't really sit around the dinner table together unless it was a religious or special occasion.

I don't really remember my parents' dynamic; I remember them quite individually. I don't recall my mum getting angry very often or arguing with my dad. What I do remember is that she was always very glamorous, very put-together, not a hair out of place and utterly immaculate. As I said, appearance and how things looked on the outside seemed very important in our family. Image was key. If the outside was perfect, perhaps it didn't so much matter what was going on underneath the surface. I'm not sure my parents were even together that much in the house because my dad was out at work.

While Mum was quite measured, Dad was very colourful. My dad had a great sense of humour, and was a big energy in every room he walked into – captivating, engaging and so much fun. I definitely share his sense of humour. He was also the one I'd go to if I wanted a bit of reassurance or a cuddle. It wasn't like we had the kind of relationship where I'd sit and talk to him about my thoughts and feelings, just that I'd tend to go to him if something upset me.

I've seen pictures of my parents when they were young, and they were such a beautiful couple – movie-star beautiful. In fact, anyone I've ever spoken to about them has said what a good-looking couple they were.

Still, it's hard for me to give a complete or vivid picture of my parents' upbringing and background because I've only ever known fragments of their family history. It's only now that I'm putting the pieces together myself and learning who they really are. The more I grow, the more I understand them.

I never met my grandparents on my dad's side. They both died quite young. My dad told me recently that when his father died, his mum, distraught and devastated, moved to Australia, but she passed away not long after. My Papa Alan died when I was eight, so Grandma Pearl, on Mum's side was the only grandparent in our lives. Grandma Pearl, always so glamorous, with her bright-red hair, and the leopard-print walking stick she never wanted to use. She was always so cool – right to the end of her life – and she had the most wonderful sense of humour.

Over the years, Mum has told me bits and pieces about her background and my dad's history, including a few things that didn't surprise me, knowing my dad as I do now. She once told me that Dad would often exaggerate about what he had and how and where he lived to outsiders, and even some friends, to make out he was richer and more successful than he was. What I've taken from that is that perhaps he was not as confident as he made out. Perhaps he never felt like the real him was good enough, although that's not for me to say. From what Mum says, his parents idolised him, but although they showered him with external praise and adoration, I wonder if there was enough focus on what was going on inside.

Still, I could see why people gravitated towards my dad; he had a magnetism that captivated people. I adored him when I was young; I suppose you could say I idolised him, just like his parents had. But it didn't last. Everything would soon change, and I could never have imagined what that change would be.

Chapter 2

OVERTHINKING

I'VE ALWAYS BEEN incredibly sensitive. As a child, I could always sense when something was going on, even if it was being kept from me. This meant that I grew up with a constant underlying uncertainty, which often left me feeling on edge and unsafe.

Despite the importance placed on the external in our family, I grew up thinking and feeling very deeply about things. I always had questions – at least, in my head; I just didn't have anywhere to direct them. Consequently, that's where I spent most of my time – in my head. I was a deep thinker and a worrier, and with no outlet for those thoughts and worries, I suffered with serious anxiety. This anxiety initially manifested as a fear of being sick. Emetophobia is an extreme fear of vomiting, seeing others vomit, or even feeling sick. For me, it's always been about control – or the lack of it. When you're being sick, you can't control how you look or what happens. You can't be composed. It's simply about purging and letting go – two things that were always scary to me.

This phobia started off when I was about eight or nine, but it's something I've really struggled with throughout my life. As a child, I wouldn't sleep over at friends' houses because of it, and there were certain foods I avoided. It really took a strong hold over my life. The anxiety was always present.

It got to the stage where if ever I felt slightly unwell, I'd have a panic attack, thinking I was going to be sick and lose control. It was horrible. This was one of the things I'd go to my dad about. It helped to have reassurance and distraction in those insecure and scary moments.

Mum took me to a couple of therapy sessions when I was still quite young – because of my panic attacks and emetophobia. It was just a couple of sessions, but it wasn't an ongoing or consistent support. It would have been interesting to see how it might have helped me if I'd continued, but as we all know it was a very different time. I was a sensitive and emotional child and I think they found me hard to deal with and to understand. I can see that now, and also I can relate to it. I find it challenging, as a parent, to deal with my own emotions while trying to give my daughters what they need. I know how important it is to be emotionally connected to your children. You have to be, so you can help them develop in a healthy way.

Childhood anxieties aside, there were many happy times when I was a child, moments I still remember fondly and cherish. One of my favourite memories was our family holiday when we drove to Rimini, in Italy, when I was nine or ten. We didn't go on many foreign holidays because, as I found out later, Dad had a fear of flying (one of a few fears my dad had that I picked up along the way). Also, we couldn't really afford to regularly go abroad in those days.

It was such an adventure, driving through so many different landscapes on the journey there. I recall tasting incredible Italian food for the first time, the balmy air, and the excitement of being away with my family. I also happened to meet a very cute boy, who caught my eye at a hotel we were staying in and was about my age. Much too young for anything to come of it, of course, but we'd stare dreamily across the dining room at one another during mealtimes.

It was a special time away, and a real adventure. Even Grandma Pearl came along for the ride!

I'd always had a strong determination to see the world and a sense of excitement about what might be out there. I thought about just how big the world was, and all the many possibilities ahead of me. No matter what might stand in my way, I wanted to experience life, and nothing was going to stop me.

The thing I cherish most about that holiday, apart from time with my family and the food, was the laughter. My dad always knew how to make us laugh; he had that wonderful gift. In fact, that's one of the things I remember most about being a kid. One of my clearest and funniest memories of the journey was us driving through the mountains. For a start, Mum had to crouch on the floor of the car because she was scared of heights and couldn't look out of the window. At the top of the mountain, we stopped to admire the amazing view, but when my dad opened the car door, my grandma fell out of it onto the ground. We were all hysterical – the whole experience was like a comedy sketch.

In joyful times like that, I could have been anywhere. When you're a child, you don't really care about the grand stuff; you just want happy times with the people you love. We might have been holidaying in Italy, but we could just as well have been having dinner together at Biguns Ribs, the long-gone American-style diner chain. That was one of my favourite nights out. We regularly went there for dinner, and when I think about it now, it makes me think of family, which meant everything to me back then. I remember thinking, I want to be just like my mum when I grow up and marry someone like my dad; I really looked up to them both. In fact, my happiest memories from my early childhood came from the simplest things – being together, eating out together, laughing. Everything bubbling happily away on the surface, nothing dark or troubling. I craved that simple connection when I was a child – I guess we all do.

I was always amazed at how glamorous my mum was. On nights out with Dad, she always looked so well put-together and smelled of the perfume she still wears today. She instilled good values in me and taught me to always do the right thing. Growing up, she made sure we always had nice dinners, saw our friends, went to summer camps, and she always came to see me in my school performances, even when I wasn't doing all that much. I was always better and more interested in the dancing and music side of things than I was in acting. If ever I was in a school play, there was never any major dramatic role involved. I was more likely to be cast as a tree with a costume that had been thrown together the night before the show. One performance that stands out was with hundreds of us, all dancing to Michael Jackson's 'Smooth Criminal' in a school field. That was brilliant fun, and, of course, Mum was there to see me among the masses of other kids.

As I've got older, so many things have unfolded. Things I didn't know about that happened between my parents, which have opened my eyes to the fact that, at times, Mum was simply holding on for dear life, trying to keep it all together.

I was fifteen when my parents separated. It was a significant life event, you might think, but this was just another case of nobody saying anything about anything. No one sat us down and told us what was about to happen, despite the enormity of the situation. One minute Dad was there, living in our house, and the next, he was gone. We were a family one day, and then we weren't. Overnight it all changed, and if I'm honest, that period of my life is all a bit of a blur.

After the separation, things changed drastically. For a start, I don't remember seeing much of my dad. We lost our family home in Southgate because Mum couldn't afford to keep it up on her own. So we moved into a rented house in Cockfosters, not too far away, although life was suddenly very different. Dad would come around every now and again, but there was never any special dedicated or structured time for us to see him. I didn't go for dinners with him or spend time on my own with him to do nice father–daughter things. I only saw him when he popped over unannounced, which might be every week or every few weeks.

I willed myself not to feel anything about my dad having left; I was numb. I'd been so conditioned into hiding or squashing my emotions, I didn't really know how to express my confusion or even experience my sadness anyway. So I just shut it all down, I pulled it inside. It's strange, because if I felt something physically, like a panic attack, I could get my head around that feeling and talk about it and control it, but emotions or anything that came from the soul were puzzles not to be discussed or acknowledged.

What I did feel was that the rug had been pulled from under my feet when Dad left. It was limbo. My mum, bless her, must have been going through hell because I now know that at that time my dad was having a serious affair. He had another life that none of us knew about, and it had been going on for some time. When Mum eventually found out about the affair, she was, of course, devastated, but when she eventually told my dad she was willing to try to repair their marriage, he told Mum that his girlfriend was pregnant with his child. After that, there was no going back. At the time, Mum didn't tell me what she knew, so it was a while before I'd discover I had a new sibling. It must have been so incredibly hard for her, knowing all that but keeping it from us. Maybe she thought she was, in some way, protecting us.

Instead of pulling together as a family after the split, we all found our different coping strategies and ways of getting through it all. My brothers and I were at an age where we could be more independent, so while they were out and about with their friends, I was out with mine, pretending everything was OK and pushing down all my feelings. We were fragmented, residing in this strange new house that felt nothing like home. This was the stark reality of our new family situation.

Mum, meanwhile, became distant, lost in her own private grief. Although she did her very best to protect us, her way of doing that was not to talk about anything. After a while, she wasn't around much either. She was also in shutdown. She was often out, doing her own thing, understandably, trying to make a new life for herself. Even when she was at home physically, she wasn't there emotionally. Looking back, I know she was simply trying to take in what had happened after her life had been turned upside down. Mum still touches on her absence during that time every so often.

I have compassion for why she was the way she was. She'd lost her husband and her home, and dealt with it in the best way she knew. My mum is and always has been a kind, amazing woman from whom I've taken so many good qualities. I feel like, at that time, Mum struggled to share her nurturing, emotional side, which I needed more than anything, but, I guess, so did she. I've had to do a lot of work on myself to understand how my relationship with my mum and dad has affected me.

Thankfully, Mum eventually met a lovely man called Russell, who became my stepdad. They're still married, twenty years on.

My relationship with my dad all but disintegrated after he left. It was like I didn't even know him anymore, and I didn't know his new girlfriend either. As time went on, it felt to me like he became a stranger, and we were distant and disconnected. That hadn't been my decision, far from it. He was absent, I felt abandoned, and I missed having my dad terribly. I was beyond heartbroken; I just didn't know what to do with those feelings. I didn't know how to process the grief, which is what it felt like. The love I'd had for my dad as a child was my truest love, and when it went away, I was numb. It was the catalyst that would lead to my own emotional shutdown. It wasn't just the loss, either; there were many things he did afterwards that broke my heart.

These days, I can detach from those feelings of hurt to a certain extent, and because I've done a lot of soul searching

and growing personally, I can feel compassion and understand some of what happened from his side. Even though
you never forget, I've learned how important it is in life to
forgive.

Chapter 3

GROWING PAINS

ONE OF THE ways in which I coped and brought happiness into my life after Dad left was nurturing the small friendship group I had outside of school. With them, I remedied my sadness with humour. Back then, I loved to watch comedy, in particular Lee Evans, or just dance and be silly to the music of the era, laughing with my friends until it hurt.

These were people I could be myself with and open up to, and one of my closest friends was Nikki. We were nine or ten when we first met, but we already knew of one another's families, just as the whole community seemed to know everyone else's family. The North London Jewish community was small, so everyone knew everybody's business.

Nikki was my safe person, the one I could be silly and myself with. We shared the same sense of humour, and I had no fear about what I said or how I behaved around her. I felt comfortable with Nikki, and she was as accepting of me as I was of her. No judgement.

In many ways we were quite different. While I was into hair, make-up and fashion, Nikki couldn't be bothered with all that; she just loved having fun and hanging out. Somehow, though, we just clicked, and we loved being together: talking, eating, socialising and laughing (this is still the case, well into our forties). The fact that we were so relaxed around one another meant our friendship was important to both of us. It was solid and safe, despite our differences.

On Thursday nights, we went to a youth club called Os & Gs – Oxford and St George's. I lived for those Thursday nights. This was a place where we could mix and socialise with friends our own age, which was something I loved to do.

We hung out, and played music and games of spin the bottle with the boys – all very innocent, of course.

I always felt much more connected to that group of kids than I did to the ones at school. It was like a fresh start, an opportunity to be with a group of friends I could call my own. I still felt like a bit of an outsider some of the time, but I was definitely happier and more at ease with them. I was excited that this seemed to be the start of a bigger friendship circle, but I only let a few get close.

Looking back, I think keeping a slight distance from others was my way of protecting myself. So, I was in but not in. Nikki stuck by me, which is without doubt the reason we're still friends today. If it had been left to me, we'd have probably drifted apart. Not because I didn't love her or care, I just grew up finding it hard to trust in relationships or friendships. Often, I didn't believe they would last because, up until that point, a lot of people in my life had been transitory. They came, and they went. Nikki has broken the mould by sticking around. It's a friendship based on laughter and unconditional love, and I'm truly grateful for that.

Talking to me just the other day, she told me how grown up she thought I was in our youth-club days, with my little handbag and lip gloss, and noting I always had a packet of Polos in my bag. In truth, I had them because any time I was anxious, I'd have a Polo, which was like a security blanket. Down the line, my fellow S Clubbers always made fun of me because I'd gone from Polos to Tic Tacs, and I would rattle everywhere I went. Eventually, they gave me the nickname 'Rats', which they still call me to this day.

While I got on better with the kids at Os & Gs, I still had some underlying issues with girls being bitchy, and sometimes even boys could be mean and unkind. At a friend's house, during one of our 'evenings in', as we called them, some of the boys decided to throw me into the pool with all my clothes on – at least, that was their plan. I'd seen them all whispering, and I got the feeling they wanted to somehow single me out, which felt horrible and uncomfortable. Consequently, even in groups I felt relatively comfortable around, it got to the stage where I was always on high alert. Always waiting for someone to do or say something mean or unkind – although I certainly wasn't going to let that stop me from going out and enjoying a social life.

As a teenager, I was often left to my own devices. When Nikki and I hung out together, we'd head to the local Chinese takeaway and pick up chow mein – just one between the two of us. Neither of us ever had money, right through our teenage years. We'd forever be digging around down the cushions of the sofa to find any loose change that might have fallen out of somebody's pocket. A chow mein to share and an evening of backgammon was usually on the cards when Nikki and I hung out together.

Eventually, I wanted to start earning my own money, for essentials like clothes, make-up and chow mein, so I got a Saturday job in a shoe shop in Southgate called Samana. Obviously, I ended up spending most of my wages buying shoes from the shop, so I still starved, but at least I had nice shoes.

My love of clothes and fashion grew as I grew. My uniform at that time was a sweetheart-neck body, always black, and high-waisted jeans, or baggy combat trousers, and perhaps Chipie or Chevignon or Fila trainers. That was after my fluorescent ra-ra skirt, cycling shorts and perm era in the mid- to late Eighties, which was followed by the oversized-T-shirt, baggy phase.

My curiosity around beauty and make-up also grew around that time. From a young age, I was always experimenting, making lotions, potions and perfumes in the bathroom with flowers from the garden and powders and creams from the bathroom cabinet. Unfortunately, some of my beauty experiments led to some questionable eyebrow incidents. At certain points, I was quite tweezer-happy! In fact, you could map the evolution of my eyebrows through the timeline from my teenage years onwards – they had their own personality. I longed to have brows just like Kate Moss's. I butchered them to within an inch of their life to achieve this and looked nothing like Kate Moss at the end of it. Not pretty!

Eyebrow butchering aside, I wasn't especially rebellious back then. I don't think I had anything to rebel against. I was never grounded and I don't remember anyone saying no to me. I didn't go in for underage drinking or getting up to things I wasn't supposed to. Having emetophobia was probably the biggest reason I've always shied away from the idea of getting drunk, and drugs were completely off the table. I always wanted to stay in control, so even when I did go out with friends as I got older, I'd always offer to be the driver. Consequently, I've never been drunk – well, not really. I've been nicely tipsy, warm and fuzzy, but never falling-down drunk. And these days, I don't need or want to be. That said, I think it's important to be able to let go and, yes, perhaps be a little out of control sometimes. Letting go is something I've always struggled with.

During my teenage years I always thought of myself as a little social butterfly. It was a very different time, with no mobile phones, so plans were made on the doorstep or on a landline, and once you were out you were out. My parents knew my friends and trusted me, so I pretty much had a free rein, with no constraints.

At the time, I loved and appreciated that freedom, and the idea that I didn't really have anyone to answer to. I knew my mum was there if I needed her, and I had a roof over my head, but there were no real boundaries. But writing this, it's becoming very apparent that I never really had any solid boundaries. I think a few more rules and some structure might have helped me feel safe and supported. As we know, parenting isn't just making sure there's food on the table; boundaries are a way of nurturing, caring and showing love, too.

Outside the safe space of my group of friends, the bullying I experienced didn't stop at school. To varying degrees, it filtered through to almost every social group I was a part of, and it mainly came from other girls. It ranged from nasty comments and bitchiness to me being punched in the face, and everything in between. The punch in the face came because I went out with a boy that another girl also happened to like. In fact, I was punched by three different girls on three different occasions, two of them over boys.

On one occasion, we were hanging around in Golders Green outside a café called the Filling Station, which is what we used to do back then, when one girl was being particularly mean to me – in my face, aggressive and provoking. I don't even remember what it was about. My older brother Jason clocked what was going on and went to talk to the girl's brother.

'Can you have a word with your sister?' he asked politely. 'She's giving Rachel a hard time.'

Before I knew it, the girl's brother was attacking Jason and a fight broke out. Not only that, but the brother's friends decided to join in and go for Jason. What they failed to realise was that Jason had a black belt in kung fu and had no worries when it came to looking after himself. Consequently, I stood there watching as, one by one, Jason's attackers went flying outwards and downwards onto the pavement. He'd never have started a fight, but he certainly knew how to end one.

Still, I never stopped trying to be sociable and to make friends. When a group of girls from my youth club organised a shopping trip, I was happy to have been included in the plans. Aged twelve or thirteen at the time, I was excited to be going into town with this group of girls, probably because I saw them as cool and popular, or perhaps it was just because I wanted them to like me. My dad drove me to the station to meet them, but when I got there, they'd already left without me. They'd known I was coming, it was arranged, but someone had obviously suggested, 'Let's go without her,' and the rest had followed suit. Either that, or they'd planned it that way all along, telling me that I could join them on their shopping excursion while having no intention of letting me. It doesn't sound like much, but that experience was incredibly crushing for me as a child – the thought that nobody in that group liked or cared enough about me to stand up and say, 'No, let's wait for Rachel.'

On another occasion, I was hanging out with my friends when a group of girls I knew of started following us and spitting on me from behind, singing the opening lines of a Divinyls song ... 'I love myself ...'

The idea that I loved myself was so far off the mark. Growing up, I had a certain amount of inner confidence which was sadly misunderstood, so eventually, doubt started to take over. What I didn't do was walk around thinking I was something special. I saw people for who they were and how they treated others, and always wanted to see the best in everyone. Being bitchy simply wasn't in my nature. It didn't occur to me to be nasty to or about other people.

With image being such a big part of my growing up, I couldn't help but be aware of it. As I got older, it started to define me more and more, and it often came at the expense of nurturing what was inside. It was how I learned to express myself, so I was always well turned out, with perfect make-up, and, because of my ever-growing love of fashion, nice clothes. I think that's where the problem came for me. Others saw this as vanity and thought, just like the song says, that I loved myself. In truth, despite my confident exterior, I was anything but. In fact, my confidence got less and less as time went on, and, ironically, vanity became my protection and my armour.

Again, looking back as an adult and a parent, I ask myself why shouldn't we love ourselves? Why don't we grow up thinking that's OK? This is something I'm now trying to instil in my girls every day. That it's wonderful to love yourself; we need to. As long as we are decent and kind, we should be celebrating ourselves as well as others. I know it's easier said than done, and that we all grow up with our own insecurities, but we must always try to be kind to ourselves and others.

Chapter 4

SOCIAL BUTTERFLY

THE SOCIAL SCENE in North London felt huge, and there was always a large group of us hanging out together. I enjoyed being out and about, but because of the hurtful social situations I'd gone through with various girls, there was always a thread of unease running through me. I would be on my guard in case something kicked off.

Back then, aside from youth club and hang-outs, we'd all go to these teenage party events. It was about dancing the night away, having a giggle and doing typical teenage stuff, thinking we were all so grown up.

My first kiss was in a cupboard when I was twelve. It happened during a game of spin the bottle at someone's house on one of our 'evenings in'. He was a nice boy, and yes, we snogged in a cupboard.

Looking back, I liked the positive attention I got from boys. I think it it affirmed how I looked, and the importance of how I looked was getting stronger as I got older and my inner self was shutting down. It gave me some kind of validation, and boys liking the way I looked was something

I could achieve. So I had a steady stream of boyfriends from the age of about twelve. At that age I was looking for a connection, a safe place, someone I could love and who could love me back for *me*. I was always a romantic as far back as I can remember and, as cheesy as it sounds, I just love love. What I've learned about myself over time is that I was never going to find the connection I sought because, throughout my life, I never truly opened myself up to being loved – at least, not within a relationship. I never let anyone get close enough to love me.

I didn't know it then, but I met the boy I would eventually marry when we were both twelve. I met Alex Bourne at Os and Gs, and he became one of my earliest boyfriends; we were actually boyfriend and girlfriend at the time of his Bar Mitzvah. At that age, we were going to a Bar Mitzvah virtually every weekend.

I was mad about Alex, absolutely besotted. He was gorgeous, with brown, almond-shaped eyes and dark hair that fell over his forehead in cute, floppy curtains, and he was funny and cheeky. We were together as a couple for four whole weeks that first time, so yes, it was serious. Alex says that he was the one who finished with me, but, strangely, I don't quite remember it happening that way!

Looking back, our first kiss isn't what anyone would describe as glamorous or romantic – it was in the boys' toilets at Os and Gs youth club. It was all very innocent, but it was the first and last time I ever went into a boys' toilet. Unfortunately, my dad arrived to pick me up while I was mid-snog, and he was not happy to find me there. Oh my God, did I get a telling-off for that – he was so angry.

'You never go into the boys' toilet,' he screamed at me. 'Never!'

It came as a shock to me. I guess I was so naive and innocent when it came to anything about boys and romance – and certainly anything sexual. It just hadn't occurred to me that I was doing anything wrong or bad. I'd just wanted to kiss Alex, and the boys' loos had seemed private and as good a place as any to do it.

My dad often told me always to respect myself, never to let boys take advantage of me, or make me do anything I didn't want to do or feel comfortable doing. I guess being a man and knowing how some boys think, it was hard for my dad being the father of a teenage girl.

I really appreciated my dad teaching me that lesson, and I took a lot of good from it, but I also feel it added to the control I was already consumed by, which was building inside me and starting to affect other areas of my life – my anxiety, my emetophobia. The problem was, my relationship with my dad had never really gone past the father–young child stage, so he probably didn't have a grasp on how to parent me going through puberty and beyond. For this reason, his message of concern about what I was doing with boys felt slightly confusing to me. His words must have sunk in, though, because I really valued my dad's ideals. I had it firmly in my mind that if I didn't want to do certain things with a boy, I didn't have to.

My first real love was Zack. We met via the local community of kids in the area where we lived and both hung out in the same group. He was a lovely guy, and very good looking, with a great sense of humour. Zack was slightly older than me, but in many small ways, it seemed like we were meant to be together – there were definite signs. We shared the same birthday, our houses had the same door number, and our dads both had the same first name.

As I said, there had been boys before Zack, but he was, I suppose, the one I think of as my first real relationship. At sixteen, he was the first boy I fell hard for, and I still have all the letters he wrote to me. Hundreds of them. This, as far as we were concerned, was love, and we went out together for two years until I was eighteen.

We were so close that I even went on holiday with his family to the South of France. It was so exciting to go on holiday with someone that I felt so close to and safe with. We'd not been abroad much as a family, so this was a bit of an adventure, and it was nice being part of a family unit.

During the time I was with Zack, something happened that shocked me to the core. I was out with some friends at a place called the G Spot – a North London pool bar where we all hung out as teenagers, socialising, eating and doing the odd bit of karaoke.

One night, aged sixteen, I was sitting at the table there when one of the waitresses came over and smiled at me.

'You look so much like your little brother Marcus,' she said.

I looked up at her, puzzled. 'I don't have a little brother called Marcus ...'

But I did. I just didn't know it at the time. This waitress was the bearer of the news that my dad had fathered a child with his partner, who later became his wife.

I went straight outside the club to call Dad. When he answered, I asked him if it was true that he had a new son, and he told me no, he did not. I later found out that he did and it hurt. If only he'd just told me the truth. Yes, it would still have been painful, but his honesty would have felt more respectful. I know it's not always an easy thing, but we owe that to the people in our lives.

Like many things in my life, I simply chose not to feel it at the time. My relationship with my dad was such that I told myself to push the feelings away and move on. The information went in and got filed away. By now, I was so used to desensitising myself to painful feelings that it came naturally. I played down and normalised quite major traumatic events as a way of protecting myself. I understand that now. The trouble is, when stuff is internalised for too long, it's a mess that's hard to unravel when you finally attempt to.

Now, Marcus is about to turn thirty, and although we don't see him regularly, he is a sweet and lovely man, as is his younger brother Brandon. Marcus is always trying to bring the family together, and over the years he has always been the one who tried to get my dad and me to reconnect.

Eventually, Dad married his girlfriend, but at the time I never knew anything about it, and I wasn't invited to the wedding. It was strange finding out about that, as Dad's new wife, Kristina, was only ten years older than I was. Looking back, it feels odd that neither of us felt like the news of him marrying was an important enough thing for him to tell me or for me to want to know.

After that, the connection between my dad and I got weaker. I'm not sure he knew how to bond with me as a young woman, given that he'd left when I was a teenager. He was used to me looking up to him and idolising him, but as I got older, that dynamic naturally changed and he didn't seem to know how to deal with that.

My avoidance of the trauma of all that was probably one of the reasons why, after Zack, I was always in one relationship or another. Subconsciously, I think I was trying to avoid pain and loneliness. Consequently, I found myself staying with partners for much longer than I should have, knowing that they weren't right, simply because I would rather be with someone than be on my own.

Chapter 5

MUSIC, PASSION AND EVERYTHING FASHION

THERE WAS ALWAYS music in our house, all the greats: Prince, Michael Jackson, Madonna, Elvis – my brother was a massive Elvis fan. My dad was really into music too when I was little, so I was very much influenced by his favourites. I loved going out in the car with him, radio blaring. Dad loved soul music – Motown, Teddy Pendergrass. He also loved Simon & Garfunkel – music with gorgeous melodies and harmonies. I also loved a good power ballad, something you could really belt your heart out to. Then, in the late Eighties and early Nineties, I became (and still am) a huge Kylie Minogue fan, and I may or may not have had a Jason Donovan poster in my bedroom. I also loved soul and R&B – so I took bits from all of it.

In early 1990, Mum took me to a Kylie Minogue concert at the London Arena. I'd just turned twelve. During the show, I watched Kylie doing her thing, mesmerised. At one point, I turned to Mum and said, 'I'm going to do that one day.'

I really believed it, and Mum clearly remembers me saying it. I have always been a great believer in manifesting things in your life. I think if you really want something and really believe it can happen, there's a good chance it will.

Although I loved singing, I didn't know if I was any good. I knew I wasn't terrible, but I certainly had no illusions of being able to do it professionally. Growing up, Nikki had been my only audience. Throughout our teenage years, I'd tell her I was going to sing for her, but she had to turn around and face the other way – she wasn't allowed to watch while I was performing. Little did I know that, one day, my audience was going to grow quite considerably, and I wouldn't be able to ask them all to turn around. Being the good friend that she was, Nikki was always very supportive and complimentary, but that wasn't enough to convince me I was good enough to do it professionally.

I'm not sure if my parents realised just how much I loved singing, but it certainly wasn't nurtured in any way. Consequently, my singing stayed very much in the bedroom, and I suppose for a long time, I thought it was something that would remain untapped. It never crossed my mind that performing might be a career path. As far as that went, it was fashion and clothes all the way.

I shared my love of fashion with my mum and my grandma, who were both very stylish. When I was little, Wednesday would always be the day when Mum spent time with Grandma. They would often go shopping together and sometimes buy things for me, laying them out on the bed for me to see when I got home from school. I remember being so excited trying the items on, doing a little fashion show.

My grandma even managed a high-end fashion boutique in Staines, so I used to go there to check out what she had on the rails. At age eight, I would wander around, taking in the smell and feel of the fabrics, learning what went together. The shop was pretty opulent, with its thick green 1970s carpet, and I shared the joy the customers had when they came into the boutique.

I enjoyed the fact that my grandma and my mum were glamorous women. They both had this incredible sense of taste and quality. It's not that they were wealthy enough to afford the best; it was just that they had excellent style and, of course, placed a great deal of importance on presentation.

At age twelve, I entered a hair modelling competition in *Just 17* magazine, which was a popular teen mag of the day. My mum sent in pictures of me and four girls were chosen to have their hair done in a top salon and have photos taken – a sort of before-and-after type thing. It was a day out in London and very exciting.

When I told other kids at school about the competition, I got a lot of stick from the girls. They asked me who I thought I was, and when I took the magazine to school, it was a case of, 'Who cares?' Still, I didn't let it faze me. I was so proud of what I'd achieved and enjoyed my moment in front of the camera.

As I got older, I read all the fashion mags I could get my hands on. I loved watching *The Clothes Show* on TV and sometimes went to *Clothes Show Live* events. I wasn't super knowledgeable about all the designers at that time; I just loved the glamour and atmosphere of that world. I was obsessed with all the Nineties supermodels – Cindy Crawford, Linda Evangelista and Christy Turlington. It was a world I wanted to be a part of.

At one of the *Clothes Show Live* events, when I was about fifteen, I was approached by a woman who told me she worked for Models 1, which was, and still is, one of the most successful and respected modelling agencies in the world.

'Would you be interested in coming over to our stall to have your photograph taken?' she asked.

I couldn't believe it – me at five-foot-nothing! Of course, I didn't have to be asked twice, so off I went to have a Polaroid or two taken. From there, I was invited into the Models 1 offices for a chat. Unfortunately, that's as far as it went. At my height, I was never going to be gracing the catwalk at major fashion shows. Still, the idea that I'd even been chosen to have my photograph taken and invited in to meet with a modelling agency was exciting, and I knew it meant something. I just wasn't sure what.

When I was seventeen, I got into the London College of Fashion, which was the one thing I always knew I wanted to do. I didn't require any significant academic qualifications to get in, which was fortunate. I'd passed all my GCSEs, but I was pretty much an average C student across the board through school – only taking a serious interest in art and history. There wasn't much in the way of music and drama at my school either, so those were the only two subjects I took seriously. I never had any interest in going to university; what I really wanted was to get out there into the workplace.

When I started at LCF, I didn't really know what part of the industry I was aiming for. Thinking I might make a good fashion buyer, I chose a business course along with my friend Sasha. She was a friend from my Os and Gs days; we shared a love of fashion, so we both applied for the course together, and we both got accepted. Being with Sasha made the idea of college even more fun. I was still living at home, but I often stayed over at her place, talking and laughing into the night, and planning our futures. We loved clothes shopping, entered the odd modelling competition together and even did a photo session together – our first real fashion shoot – for a guy we met who had a modelling agency. I don't see Sasha all that often these days, but there's still closeness and a special friendship between us now.

I suppose being at LCF had been our first taste of being out in the world as young women, away from the restrictions of school but without the responsibilities of work.

Unfortunately, though, the course never matched up to its promise, and I now couldn't for the life of me tell you what

I learned. I've since spoken to other people that were on my course who felt the same. I seem to remember spending more time in the coffee shop in Bond Street tube station with Sasha than I did in a college classroom.

The other major problem I had with LCF was the tube journey to get there. I hated tube travel and the idea of being underground because of my claustrophobia. I'd once had a severe panic attack when a tube train got stuck in a tunnel – it was as if the walls of the carriage were closing in on me; it was such a horrible experience.

Another time, I was on a tube late at night with Sasha when a group of rowdy older kids piled on and sat on the seats facing us. There were a mix of guys and girls, and when I say kids, they were late teens/early twenties, but noisy and quite aggressive. They were making fun of us and trying to intimidate us, and it worked. At the next available stop, Sasha and I both got off and ran for it. I remember the feeling of relief at the tube doors opening and the freedom of jumping off. I hated the idea of being stuck on there with no way of getting off. That was a real turning point for me, the idea that there might be a danger-ous situation that I couldn't get away from. After those two incidents, my fear of being underground or in a small space just got worse.

My other fear with claustrophobia is the fear of getting in a lift, which comes from the knowledge that if I get stuck in one, I can't get myself out – I have to rely on someone else.

But I had a plan to get around my tube fear when travelling to LCF: I just needed a car. I couldn't wait to take my driving test and get on the road. I was desperate for that independence the moment I turned seventeen. I took lessons as soon as I could – luckily there was no theory test back then – and the minute my instructor and I thought I was ready, off I went to apply for my test. It didn't take me too many tries to pass, but if you are going to fail, you might as well make it an epic fail. And my first fail was indeed epic! It started off so well: hold the wheel at ten to two, mirror, signal, manoeuvre. I was smashing it figuratively, and then, quite literally when I crashed into a parked car. It was a shock, and I was so upset. Still, we move on, and a few weeks later I took the test again and passed.

Once I was finally on wheels and on the road, I could drive to Stanmore to get to college and hop on the Jubilee line, because that meant I only had to go into the tunnel for a few stops. It wasn't ideal, but it was the best solution I could think of.

Post fashion college, I worked for a couple of PR companies, making tea and running errands, but those jobs were fleeting. Aside from my love of clothes and design, I was also intrigued by the entertainment world, so I applied for a receptionist job at a film production company near Baker Street. I was nervous but still confident going to the interview. My attitude was, yeah! I'm going to get this job! I suppose I was quite streetwise at that age. I think that's something I picked up from my dad. He was always a bit of a Del-boy, a wheeler-dealer, and I obviously learned from him how to hustle and put myself out there. As a result, I went into the interview with positive energy, and got the job.

I was so excited, going out to buy my first ever suit from Karen Millen – a proper working-girl look – and once I started, I enjoyed having a structure to my day. I loved getting into the office and putting the coffee on, then sitting down at the desk and preparing for a day of making appointments and fielding calls. This was something that was mine, something I'd achieved on my own. I was proud of myself.

I ended up being at the film company for about a year, and as far as I was concerned, I was pretty good at my job. Down the line, however, someone I'd worked there with told me, 'You're a much better popstar than you were a receptionist.'

I never earned much, and every bit of money I did have was still going on clothes. I'd skimp on food and petrol for the car, putting in the bare minimum so that I had more to spend on outfits. Nikki and I once put just two pounds' worth of petrol in my car, because that's all I could afford. It still got us to where we were going, though!

At that time, my younger brother Leigh worked in the canteen at the Sony Music offices, which were nearby, so I could often get a free lunch. He worked there alongside my dad's new wife, Kristina, who'd helped him get the job there – my brothers were much more a part of my dad's life than I was, which was sometimes difficult for me. Back then, hearing about some of the things they did together that I missed out on was hard.

It was in the Sony canteen where I got my introduction to the music industry. It was one of those sliding-door, right-place, right-time moments you hear about, and where my whole S Club journey began. I was just sitting there, eating my lunch, when I was approached by two guys who introduced themselves and told me they were record producers. Their names were Mike Rose and Nick Foster – collectively known as the Dufflebag Boys or just Rose and Foster – and they asked me if I could sing.

'Yes, I can sing,' I said, despite still not really knowing if I was any good.

It didn't even cross my mind to say otherwise. If nothing else, I was always extremely driven. As far as I was concerned, if an opportunity was being presented, I was going to grab it with both hands.

It turned out Mike and Nick were working on a brand-new music project – a pop artist called Lolly. They'd written and produced some tracks but, as yet, hadn't found anyone to front the project – to actually be Lolly. Having spotted me in the Sony canteen, they wondered if I might be the girl for the job.

The project was for Polydor Records, and not long after that chance meeting, I ended up in the studio with Mike and Nick recording a song called 'Telephone Boy'.

Although I'd never been in a recording situation before, I think I pretty much took it in my stride. I just put on my headphones, stepped up to the microphone and sang the song until they were happy with it. It was a real bubble-gum-pop song, but at the same time, quite kitsch and fun. I enjoyed it and it seemed to go well; at least Mike and Nick both seemed happy with my performance.

For me, it was an opportunity, and I was going for it – just to see where it took me. I hadn't spoken to anyone in any great depth about what I was doing. That was the contradiction in me, I suppose. I always had this inner fire, but when something wonderful or exciting happened, I just moved through it without fully taking it in. I was positive but realistic as far as expectations went.

Once I'd recorded the song, Mike and Nick took the project to Simon Fuller at 19 Management, who'd looked after, among many other successful artists, the Spice Girls. After seeing my picture and hearing me sing, Simon had other ideas for me. During the summer of 1998, Simon invited me to a big World Cup party he was hosting at a London hotel. At the time, he was putting together a brand-new pop band, although I knew nothing about all that. I was just excited to be getting the chance to sing, and potentially release my own record – as Lolly!

I think I ended up going to Simon's World Cup party with my brother Leigh, and while I was there, I had a chat with him for about fifteen or twenty minutes before he disappeared off to mingle with his other guests. There was nothing especially in-depth about our conversation, but he was very friendly. Two weeks later, I got an unexpected call from him.

'I'm putting together a new band, and I'd like you to be a part of it,' he said. 'Do you think that's something you'd be interested in?'

There was no further audition involved. My audition had been recording the Lolly track and chatting with Simon at his World Cup party, and that was it. Looking back on it now, I think, thank God I didn't have to audition. There were about 10,000 applicants after 19 Management placed an advert in *The Stage*, and hopefuls would have had to sing and dance their way through dozens of rounds of auditions before it was whittled down to a band. I'm sure I wouldn't have got in. I'd never trained as a singer or dancer, like most of the young people who were getting into bands back then. I'd never even had a singing lesson. I was literally just walking into it green, and because I'd been sitting at the right table in the right canteen.

When I told Mike and Nick about the offer to be in Simon's new band, which was to be called S Club, they were both so supportive. They clearly knew what a big thing it was and encouraged me to go for it, despite the fact that they'd be losing their Lolly.

'This is going to be huge,' Mike told me. 'You have to go for it.'

As far as their project went, another girl became Lolly, and she had five top-twenty singles and a top-thirty album. Meanwhile ... I was now in a pop band.

Chapter 6

JOINING THE CLUB

THE EASE WITH which I'd got the S Club gig had kind of been a recurring theme for me. I never studied hard at school but always did OK. At the end of my time at school, we'd had a leavers' award ceremony, where different students were awarded for the one thing they were best at – whether that be a certain subject, sport, school or social activity, or perhaps just something they excelled at or were known for. My award was '*je ne sais quoi*' – having a certain quality that cannot be described or expressed. Literally, 'I don't know what.' It was such a random accolade, but the only one I had. So, yes, there must have been some inner self-belief there, and it was something others saw in me too.

After school, I'd got into LCF without any significant qualifications, I'd walked into jobs relatively easily, and now here I was, being invited to join a pop band by one of the most prominent managers in the entertainment business without even having auditioned.

I guess that's why, down the line, I sometimes felt a bit unqualified being in S Club. Most of the other members had either gone through some kind of stage or drama school or been involved in youth theatres. Bradley, I think, came out the womb performing, and his parents were in the music industry, so he grew up in the entertainment world. Despite knowing I had a decent singing voice, I was constantly suppressing the feeling that I'd got the gig because of how I looked rather than what I could do. OK, so maybe not just how I looked, but also how I came across, my confidence. I must have had something that drew Rose and Foster and then Simon Fuller to me, but it wasn't my singing or dancing ability. Those are things I got to showcase later down the line.

By the time I was offered the job, other members had already been cast. Jon, Hannah and Paul were the first in, then came Tina. I was the fifth member – originally, it was going to be a five-piece. Once I was in, a bonding process started, where we all hung out together and did a few dance rehearsals at Pineapple Studios. In fact, the first band member I met was Hannah – in the toilets at Pineapple; I remember thinking how cute she was.

I was still living at home, but Paul and Hannah shared a flat together in the early days, as they'd known one another from both being in the National Youth Music Theatre, so a few of us would sometimes spend time there. Hannah was close friends with Sheridan Smith, so she'd also hang out there with us. All of them were involved in the singing, acting or dancing worlds in some way, but it was such a different world for me. Still, it was a good way for us all to bond and get to know one another. A little way down the line, two more members were added – Jo and Bradley. And then we were seven!

We all had our strengths in the band – Jon had trained at Sylvia Young and was such a great all-rounder, Hannah and Paul had theatre and musical backgrounds, Tina was from a dance background. With the addition of Jo and Bradley, we got Jo's powerhouse of a voice – she really was the voice of the band – and Brad's cool soulful voice and energy. All bases were covered, which is exactly what Simon wanted.

Once we were a complete band, we were all invited to Simon's house in Positano on the Amalfi Coast. It was a stunningly beautiful place; a maze of pastel-coloured buildings stacked on a hillside above a glistening blue sea. I'd never experienced anything like it, and Simon's house was like nowhere I'd ever stayed. It was a beautiful Italian villa, but minimalist in style and incredibly chic.

While we were there, Simon took us all out on a boat, and we all jumped off and swam with a fantastic backdrop of the coast in the distance. He also took us to Capri, where we went shopping around the stylish stores of Capri town, and where Simon bought us all gifts. We all got to choose something we loved, and you won't be surprised to hear that I chose shoes. Gucci shoes, to be precise; gorgeous, black, high-heeled mules with the Gucci emblem on them – chic and understated.

At Simon's villa one evening, he announced to us that the seven of us were to be the band: now called S Club 7. I guess we'd all sort of hoped that might be the case, but it hadn't ever really been made official, so there was always a bit of a question mark. Now it was certain, and we were all over the moon – so excited for the adventure to begin.

It had been a few months since meeting Simon at the World Cup party, and it would probably be a few more before things really started to happen, but fortunately we were all paid a retainer, so there was money coming in. This would have been great had I been any good with money, but I was always terrible. It would come in, and it would disappear. I'd never really been taught to budget, so there was never any forward planning.

When we signed our contract at the 19 Management offices everything suddenly felt real and incredibly exciting. What was also rather thrilling that day was the fact that we were going to get our first big pay cheque. After that, it was all a bit of a whirlwind really. Suddenly, we had a legal team and accountants – everything was done for us right from the beginning. Our only task was to be S Club 7 and to record our album, even though none of us knew what that might sound like at this stage. To be honest, I can't imagine it being any other way back then. We were very young – I was nineteen, but the youngest of us, Jon, was sixteen – and none of us had any experience in this brand-new world of the music business. Simon's team at 19 organised everything – something we learned to get used to very quickly.

One of the first things we did as a band, in late 1998, was travel up to Sheffield each weekend to record our first album with producer Eliot Kennedy. His studio, Steelworks, was based there, and we spent a lot of time working with him and his team, which included Mike Percy and Tim Lever, who'd previously been in the Eighties band Dead or Alive. The song 'Bring It All Back' was always going to be our first single, but when we first heard it, it was just an idea – a backing track with melody ideas and a great chorus – so we, as a band, were able to contribute and co-write lyrical ideas.

How ironic that the first line I got to sing in the band was, 'If people try to put you down, just walk on by don't turn around, you only have to answer to yourself.' Those words about not caring what other people think of you resonate so much with me now as an adult and as a mum. When the girls hear those lyrics I feel quite emotional because that message of self-worth is exactly what I want them, and everyone who hears it, to take to heart.

The thing I remember most about those sessions was the laughter. Jon, Jo and I share a very similar sense of humour, and Jon is one of the funniest people I've ever met, so we would always find things to be howling about in between the serious business of recording a debut album. Jo and I were like two peas in a pod, and we got close relatively quickly. As I've said, I find it hard to let people in, but with Jo, I was immediately comfortable. I felt like I could trust her. Maybe it was the new shared experience we were having – just two girls from ordinary families suddenly thrust into this fast, crazy business.

As for the recording process itself, well, I found that a bit daunting; there was definite trepidation on my part. I'd always loved music and singing, but I still didn't consider myself a real singer, certainly not in the way some of the other members of S Club were. It was one thing singing everywhere I went, or in my lounge for Nikki while she had her back to me, but singing on a record that might potentially be heard by millions of people on the radio – that was something else altogether. Part of me felt that because I wasn't trained, and hadn't had singing lessons or gone to drama school, I was a little bit out of my depth. It wasn't that I didn't deserve to be there. I'd done the recording session for the Lolly project, and that had gone well enough, but I'd been on my own for that. I wasn't in the company of six other people.

I was never very accepting of getting things wrong. I never learned how to fail. I wanted to be perfect, which is crazy because you can't be. On one occasion, in a music class at school when I was about eight, I'd wanted to play the clarinet and the teacher went around the class making all the kids sing scales with the piano. I'd never had a singing lesson or sung scales before, and I know I got something wrong or hit a wrong note somewhere when it was my turn.

'You're no good with music,' she told me, and that was the end of that. No clarinet.

That experience made me feel very vulnerable, and it's always stuck with me, that memory of getting it wrong in front of a whole classroom of kids and not being good enough. I guess that's why I was nervous about that first recording session, but over time, I got into the swing of it. We ended up recording some real S Club classics in those sessions. As well as 'Bring It All Back', we did 'S Club Party' and 'You're My Number One', which was written by the producers who'd discovered me in the Sony canteen, Rose and Foster, and 'Two in a Million', written by the legendary Cathy Dennis and the man who would eventually become our musical director, Simon Ellis.

When we were in the studio, recording, I sometimes felt an element of pressure, but, of course, I'd put the pressure on myself. When the spotlight was on me, I always had that worry about getting the melody right or hitting the notes. The band was full of talent and experience, so there was a lot to live up to.

I could dance and sing, but I never owned that fact; it would have been lovely to have given myself more credit. The thing was, it was all in my head; all my insecurities were preventing me from fully letting go and just enjoying the ride. I can see now that the idea of being perfect means nothing when it comes to being an artist. Having the most brilliant voice doesn't make somebody the best or most exciting performer. I've learned that as I've gone through my career, but it took a while. In moments of self-doubt, it can be hard to break that cycle of thought that holds you down. It's taken years of working on myself to keep those voices at bay.

The idea for S Club 7 was not just a pop band; it was a TV show, a club, a magazine, an entire brand. With all this in play, everything surrounding the group was planned and organised down to the tiniest detail.

In many ways, this was a positive thing for me. My life had felt very disjointed before S Club; I didn't feel in any way grounded or that I had much stability or structure in my life going into the band. My family were all over the place – and there was nothing approaching closeness. This was tough because family had meant everything to me when I was young, but now it just wasn't there. At least, there was no depth or foundation to it. It felt as though our family unit was so fragmented now.

When I was younger, I'd at least had a foundation of security within the family, but once the family shattered, when we'd lost our house and I'd stopped seeing my dad, there was nothing to hold on to.

Coming into S Club changed all that. For me, it was an escape from everything that had gone before. I went from never having money to receiving a regular income, and from having no family stability to this new family who were as reliant on me as I was on them. Finally, I had some direction and I felt part of something special.

Chapter 7

THE BAND BUBBLE

ONE OF OUR earliest performances as a band was a big showcase in Miami early in the summer of 1999. The management and record label flew ten journalists to Miami to meet us, see us perform and hear some of the album. This was a big deal, and a big announcement. Miami was the chosen location because that was where we were filming our first TV show, *Miami 7*.

The idea behind the show was for it to be like a modern-day version of the Monkees' TV series. (For those who might not know, the Monkees was a 1960s pop band who started off as a fictional group in a TV sitcom.) S Club was different in the fact that we were a real recording band right from the off, but the idea of the half-hour music-comedy show, with us playing heightened, exaggerated versions of ourselves and the songs from our album being featured in the show, was the same.

As exciting as it all was, I'd had a lot of anxiety about flying to Miami. I was essentially a home girl, and the idea of jetting off and leaving everything and everyone

I knew behind scared me. I knew I'd be homesick, and I was. It was eight weeks that we were away that first time, but for me, it seemed longer. Perhaps it was more the unknown that scared me; letting go of everything that was comfortable and familiar to do this big crazy thing. I knew I'd miss my mum too – she was very much my safe place.

Being close to Jo was a massive help during the Miami trip. We became one another's family away from family. I really needed that. Jo and I shared an apartment while we were in Miami, and we were practically inseparable. She was always there if I was having a wobble, as I was for her. We had a pretty full-on filming schedule, but any spare time we could grab was spent shopping together or eating out in our favourite cafés and restaurants.

The other thing I loved most about the TV show was working with the crew. I thrived on being part of a team, and it was great fun getting to know all the various people and learning about all the different jobs they did. The continuity of it all made me feel safe. I also enjoyed the table-reads, getting a first look at the script, and us all going through it together before filming started.

Although we were playing ourselves, *Miami 7* wasn't like reality TV. It was scripted with storylines, which meant a lot of work. We had scripts and choreography to learn, and the shooting schedule was full on – always very fast-paced. Most days, we were up at the crack of dawn to have our hair and make-up done, or to catch sunrises for certain scenes, and we'd often shoot late into the night.

It was a no-brainer that Miami Beach would be our backdrop for the video for our debut single 'Bring It All Back'. Being our first video shoot, we were excited and full of energy, although we knew it was going to be a long day. This was something different to our usual filming days, though; it was something special.

The video was to be intercut with scenes from the TV show, so all day we were performing our dance routine over and over again, in what felt like 100-degree heat. We might as well have been dressed in tin foil, it was so hot! On the upside, because it was the last thing we were doing on that trip, the resulting tan was timed perfectly for my upcoming twenty-first birthday back in the UK.

It was all hard work, but I thrived on it. These were exciting times; an amazing whirlwind of an experience, with highs, lows and everything in between. The future looked wonderfully bright.

Finishing that first series and coming back from Miami was a relief. I felt such a sense of warmth and comfort as I flew over London – I always loved coming home. It was also very exciting to know that everything was about to kick off; that we were about to share all our hard work with the world.

Not long after we arrived back in the UK, I had my twenty-first birthday party, in April. It was a big family affair in a West End bar, with my mum, brothers, Nikki, and a bunch of my North London friends. Mum ended up getting quite drunk that night, Nikki ended up carrying her home. Strangely, none of the band came, but that was probably because we'd all just got back and, having spent so much time in one another's company, we probably all needed a break and time to spend with our own families and friends before everything kicked off with the release of our debut single.

A few weeks later, 'Bring It All Back' was released and went straight in at number one in the UK charts, beating Madonna's 'Beautiful Stranger', which went in at number two. Eventually, the single went platinum. In July, we played our first big show, Party in the Park, in Hyde Park, alongside acts like Eurythmics, Gary Barlow, Shania Twain and Ricky Martin, among others. It had all been perfectly and strategically planned – *Miami 7* debuted in April and ran for thirteen episodes on CBBC, and the single came out in June, towards the end of the show's run. It felt huge.

Suddenly, we were everywhere. I think we must have appeared on every single kids' and music TV show going, as well as dozens of radio stations up and down the country. The biggest of them was, of course, *Top of the Pops*. At that time, and for many years before, it was the benchmark of success.

Introducing our first ever appearance, presenter Jamie Theakston said, 'I don't want to blow my own trumpet, but

I did predict that this lot would beat Madonna last week, and they look set to be the UK's next pop phenomenon.'

We were seven kids, all thrown together in this whirlwind of a well-oiled machine, living our lives in the public eye. We were under constant scrutiny, all being told to be and behave in a certain way while trying to navigate being young adults, growing and finding our feet. All with our own egos and insecurities – a minefield of teenage hormones. It was something we all dealt with in our own way. By then, certain connections had been formed, and just like with my friendship with Jo, we all tended to confide in the people we were closest to. We certainly weren't at a stage where we were talking in depth as a group about what was going on around us – there just wasn't time. With hindsight, I think we were just like any other group of teenagers would have been, thrown together in a group situation – muddling through and finding our way.

I think it dawned on me how big it had all become in the UK when I drove to Lakeside shopping centre in December 1999 to do some Christmas shopping with Nikki, and my brothers Leigh and Jason. It took us several hours to get around all the shops because people kept stopping me and asking for autographs and photos. It was lovely, but just so new and strange in that setting. Nikki told me that was the moment when everything changed – and she was right, it did.

By the time I got back from Miami, Mum had moved in to a new house with Russell, my stepdad. My brothers, meanwhile, bought a place together. Most of the time I was away working, and while I had a room at Mum and Russell's place I was hardly ever there, so nowhere really felt like home. My brothers were off doing their own thing, Mum was happy with Russell, Dad had a new family, and I was on my adventures, living out of a suitcase, in the S Club whirlwind.

By that time, my relationship with my dad had almost disintegrated. It was deeply painful for me, which meant I had to find ways to shut out that pain. I know my brothers suffered, too, but their relative closeness to my dad sometimes put a strain on my relationship with them. The trouble was, not allowing myself to feel pain caused it to manifest in other ways, such as worry and anxiety. In some respects, being in the band was a godsend. It was so all-encompassing and took up almost my entire existence. It was also offering me wonderful opportunities and experiences, so I did my best to focus on that and push the other stuff out of sight.

Aside from Jo in the band and my closest friends, my other constant during that time was my boyfriend, Daniel. He was a link to something familiar: the North London community that I'd grown up in. Daniel was another safe place; a family guy, and reliable. He was lovely and good to me, and we'd met through the group I hung out with at home before I got into the band. But feeling secure is not the best reason in the world to stay with a boyfriend; being away so much of the time made the commitment relatively easy, as much of our relationship happened over the phone or in text messages. It's much easier to turn away from the flaws in a partnership when you don't have to face them every day.

Throughout my pop career, I always seemed to have a boyfriend, whether or not they were right for me at the time. I was a big romantic. I craved a bond with someone, even if it was long-distance. Some of those relationships went on for far too long simply because I held on to them. At the point where I should have ended things, I didn't. I kept on going because I was scared of the alternative. But while I found it hard to end things, when I finally did, it was done. Finished. No grey areas or looking back.

As far as the public side of being in a pop band went, I knew I needed to be careful with my words and actions. We had a young audience, so we had to be mindful of that when talking on camera, in print or in public. I can't speak for everyone else in the band, but I felt that we were always expected to be a certain way; to uphold the clean and polished S Club image. With all that on me, it was easy to slip into the habit of keeping everything inside.

As time went on, I became more and more guarded, constantly censoring myself, especially in interviews, which I really struggled with. I found it difficult to be myself, as if

I didn't yet know who or what that was. It wasn't a conscious thing, but it felt all too exposing. With hindsight, I can see how incredibly vulnerable I was. The trouble was, I hadn't yet learned how to accept my vulnerability. It's something I'd seen in others and admired, but for me that acceptance always seemed out of reach. It's taken me a long time to allow myself to be vulnerable and know how beautiful it can be.

We had a certain amount of media training, as I assume most young pop acts did, but nothing particularly intense. Just dos and don'ts, how to present yourself and sparkle in interviews, and, more importantly, what not to say. I recall a few people close to me telling me, 'Just be yourself,' then I'd go away and feel like I'd let them down or wasn't good enough because I didn't know what that meant. When I looked at other artists, and even other members of S Club, I often wished I could be as free and natural as they appeared to be.

Time and therapy have taught me that during those many moments of vulnerability, I was carrying a sense of shame. In my mind, being my true self would be ugly. How could people accept me just being myself?

There were often times when I would even feel it physically. My voice would get stuck in my throat, or at least that's how it felt. I'd speak, but there was a panic that came with that. At the same time, if there was ever any dead space, I often wanted to fill it, because silence felt equally

My parents on their wedding
day, 1973.

The ever-glamorous
Grandma Pearl and Mum.

Baby Rachel, 1979.

Summer days.

A cute family photo!

Happy days.

With my little brother and his classic
Eighties wallpaper, 1983.

A fun sibling moment.

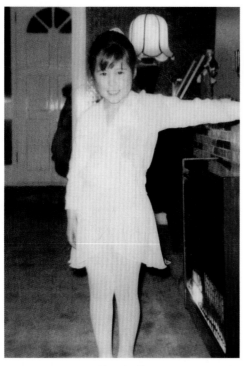

Off to ballet.

A beauty pageant, 1986.

A family holiday in
Rimini, 1988.

Ready for Alex's Bar Mitzvah, 1991.

Showcasing my love of fashion, 1991.   Continuing the modelling at home, 1994.

On set for the *Just Seventeen* shoot, 1993.

With the girls in the very early days of S Club, 1998.

With Jo and the boys.

On the streets of LA, 1999.

A happy return
home from LA.

The seven of us.

Travelling in style!

Us girls and Paul hanging out.

Our classic US wheels, 2000.

Nikki, me and my very thin eyebrows!   Miami with Jo.

With Paul and
Gayla on our trip
to Kenya, 2000.

exposing. When discussing things that I found particularly hard to get out, I felt I had to censor myself or watch what I said. It's interesting thinking and writing about that now, because I'm wondering what those subjects might have been. A lighthearted *Top of the Pops* magazine question might seem easy enough to answer, but for someone who wasn't used to being asked her opinion much, it wasn't always straightforward. Meanwhile, a more serious 'what's your opinion on this topic?' type of question threw up all sorts of problems for me. I'd have had an opinion about what I was being asked, but felt uncomfortable saying it out loud because I cared too much about what people might think of me. There was an internal panic as the question was asked.

My instinct was to want to hide away, which is ironic as I spent most of that time either in front of a camera or an audience, or in the spotlight in one form or another.

I was way out of my comfort zone in some ways, yet my release from it all was performing. It was slightly puzzling that was the case, given the conflicting emotions I carried about feeling exposed. It was as if I wanted the creative energy inside me to be seen, but at the same time I'd conditioned myself to stay in my box and not be 'too me' – whatever that was. Confusing, right? I guess it was fine for people to look at the façade – *but don't let them go any deeper*. This was relatively easy to achieve within the band because there were so many of us and everything was happening so fast. In many ways, this new life in S Club affirmed how I thought I was supposed to be and I played my role.

One of the things I was most nervous about when asked to write this book was my ability to tell a story. I never felt very good at telling stories because I didn't think people were interested in what I had to say. Sadly, I started to believe some of my own press.

As time went on, the message I got was, 'Oh, she's pretty, sweet and nice, but she hasn't got much to say for herself.'

One thing that has stuck with me for a very long time was a couple of TV presenters saying unkind things about me. One journalist commented on how hard it was to interview me. I knew in my core that it wasn't true, that I wasn't difficult, but I can understand why it might have felt that way because I was pretty much in shutdown mode. If you hear something often enough, you can sometimes question yourself and believe it. Sadly, it seems to be the case that however many positive comments we receive, it's the negative ones that stay with us. For some reason, the negative is often easier to believe. For me, it was safe and easy to stay in that lane, or at least that's what I thought. Reading or hearing people say that I didn't have much to say for myself or that I was 'a bit blah!' made me angry with myself as much as anything, because deep down, I knew I was becoming that person. As a teenager, I knew how to use my humour, and how to join in and have fun, even when I felt like an outsider.

After I got into S Club, that all changed, and it just got worse as time went on. I became more and more consumed with how I was perceived. I couldn't break free of it. It smothered me to the point where I even started to believe it myself. *Maybe it's true, maybe I don't have much to say.*

I couldn't imagine then how damaging this would all be, and just how much I'd have to unpack later in life. The truth was, I had a lot to say. I was incredibly opinionated and had so much fire and passion about so many things. I kept it all trapped inside because the alternative felt too exposing. Being passionate felt too big. Getting excited felt too scary. Being myself felt like too much.

The trouble back then was, although nothing could penetrate the walls I'd constructed, nothing could get out either. I felt so much frustration for feeling quietened, stifled and unheard. So much building up inside; all those thoughts, feelings and opinions squashed down and flattened. Eventually, it becomes toxic to body and mind, which was the case with me, resulting in a flood of anxieties and concerns, and my confidence free-falling to an all-time low.

Chapter 8

ADVENTURES
IN S CLUB

DURING OUR TIME in the band, we were given the opportunity to do things we never could have dreamed of, travelling to places we'd only ever seen on TV documentaries or in books. In the summer of 2000, we embarked on filming a TV show called *S Club 7 Go Wild!* For this, we worked with the World Wildlife Fund to raise awareness of the plight of endangered animals across the globe. The idea behind the show was that each member of S Club 7 adopted an endangered animal and then travelled to various locations around the world to their animal's natural habitat.

Full disclosure, this was not my favourite S Club experience – possibly because I'd chosen the Siberian tiger as my adoptive animal, without realising that I was going to have to fly nine hours across Russia on a very old Aeroflot plane to Vladivostok in the far east of the country.

I'd always been very anxious when out of my comfort zone, and, despite my chosen career path, wasn't great at flying long distances, or even short ones, especially in unfamiliar circumstances. True, I'd sort of got used to flying

back and forth across the Atlantic to LA on a British
Airways flight, but this was something else completely. If I
knew then what I know now, I'd have probably researched
if there were any endangered animals in Malibu or the
South of France and picked one of those. I'll admit to feeling very jealous of Hannah, who'd gone to Turkey to find a
rare seal and gone scuba diving with filming partner Bradley,
in crystal-blue waters.

Paul and I were filming partners for the series, and I'd
first flown to Kenya in search of the black rhino, which was
Paul's chosen animal. That turned out to be an amazing
trip, during which we flew over the Maasai Mara reserve in
a hot-air balloon as the sun came up, and witnessed the
wildebeest migration. The balloon landed among all the
naturally preserved Kenyan wilderness, and we ate a camp-
fire breakfast. It was stunning.

In the lead-up to my trip to Russia, I cried for two days
with nerves. When we boarded the flight from Moscow to
Vladivostok, some of my worst fears were realised. The
plane looked like it hadn't been refurbished since the
1960s. The kindest word I could use to describe it was
vintage.

I found myself fretting and thinking, *What if?* the whole
time, but I didn't feel like I could share my concerns with
Paul. He was always a quirky, live-in-the-moment type of
guy, and he didn't seem to have any issues with the uncomfortable conditions or dipping in and out of various

situations and cultures. I think deep down I was a little intimidated by that, so I felt slightly embarrassed at being such a worrier.

When we arrived in Russia, it was planes, trains and automobiles for the whole trip, just Paul, me and a small crew. Luxuries were thin on the ground, and I'm a girl who likes her home comforts. It's not that I don't like a challenge and adventure – I do! But when our management assistant, Gayla, and I noticed cockroaches scuttling about where we were sleeping one night, we weren't best pleased. Terrified one might crawl in somewhere, I covered my face, ears and mouth with gauze, just so I could get a few hours of precious sleep. I think we've established here that I'd be hopeless on *I'm a Celebrity … Get Me Out of Here!* I'd be that person the public voted for every week to do all the most horrendous trials.

We did get to see the Siberian tigers, although they weren't quite in the wild. Instead, we visited a sanctuary where I learned about the impact of poaching, and we met a family of five tigers. It was an amazing and worthy cause to bring attention to, but I was very happy when that plane landed back safely on UK soil.

More than anything, I loved the performance aspect of S Club 7, whether live on stage or on a TV show. At the time, Saturday-morning TV was a huge thing for kids and young teenagers, and shows like *SMTV Live*, with Ant and Dec, and *CD:UK* were so well done and addictive that older teenagers and adults enjoyed them, too. This is where I openly admit to loving the fact that Dec had a little crush on me. I remember him saying something particularly cheeky live on air – something you could probably only get away with back in the Noughties! It was always so much fun getting involved in the sketches and the games on *SMTV*. I loved being a part of that world and doing those morning shows. There was something about that time in the late Nineties and early 2000s. There was excitement in the air, particularly around pop music and entertainment. There was so much creativity, so much happening. Pop music really exploded during that time. For a long time, British music had been quite serious and a bit 'cooler', but groups like the Spice Girls had brought back pure pop in a big way, and it was suddenly OK to say you were a pop fan. It was such a golden era. I felt so lucky to be a part of it.

Doing those shows, as well as the iconic *Top of the Pops*, was when we'd bump into other bands and other popstars – we'd see them in the green room, in corridors or during rehearsals. Aside from those TV shows, S Club were, in some ways, separate from all the other pop bands on the scene. The 19 style of management meant we were very protected, and everything was micromanaged. We were in LA at the same time as Westlife, and Jo and I hung out with a few of them at the Mondrian hotel in West Hollywood.

But moments like that were quite rare as we were always on the go.

I sometimes wonder whether, following on from managing the Spice Girls who ended up going their own way, Simon wanted to do things differently and to keep things more controlled with S Club 7. While I understand that, it did mean that our schedules were set by 19, and everything was done and arranged for us.

Down the line, some of the other members of S Club certainly lived the life. They'd go out and party, and they'd explore all the things fame and success bought them. Jo and I were similar in that we tended to stay in our bubble. We understood one another and shared the same sense of humour, so we had fun together. I've always been a foodie! I love food, so whatever I did usually had to involve eating. I've never been one to go out drinking for the sake of drinking. I prefer sitting down and enjoying wine, along with food and conversation. Whenever people suggested going for a night out drinking, I'd always think, *Well, where does the food part come in?* I enjoyed dancing and music, but my favourite thing has always been conversation and connection.

After *Miami 7*, there was *LA 7*, *Hollywood 7* and *Viva S Club*, which was shot in Barcelona, plus half a dozen TV specials and a movie. I especially loved filming in LA; there was a buzz and an energy about the place. I felt it the moment I first stepped off the plane at LAX airport. It's always been a special place for me.

Most bands would record an album, do promotional campaigns, then maybe go on tour. We did all that plus the add-on of recording a TV series, which filled up the time when many artists might be having a break. It instilled in me a strong work ethic, for which I'm grateful.

Luckily, we were young and resilient, although there were elements of burnout in the band over time, despite the incredible experience we were having. Our filming schedule meant that we didn't even get to go to the BRITs when we won our two awards. In 2000, we won for Best Breakthrough Act, and in 2002, our track 'Don't Stop Moving' won Best British Single. Instead of attending, we recorded acceptance speeches via video. I can't speak for the others in the band, but I felt we often missed out on enjoying the fruits of our labours because, by the time it happened, we were off working on the next thing. There was very rarely any breathing space to stand back and say, 'Wow! Look what we've done here; let's enjoy it and indulge in the moment.'

There's a lot to be said for stopping for breath and taking it all in – but that's something I've only learned over time. When my stepdad, Russell, who worked in property, found me my first ever flat, I had such a sense of achievement – owning my very own place. The trouble was, I was so in the thick of work, I didn't take time to be fully present in that special moment.

It was a lovely flat in Hampstead – brand new, modern, with all fixtures and fittings and everything done. It never really felt like home, though, because I never made it truly mine, and I never found time to properly settle there. With life in S Club as full on as it was, my flat was simply a London base; I never added much in the way of personal touches. So, while having my own flat at twenty-two had felt important and exciting, it wasn't the home I had always craved.

I didn't mind working hard, though. In fact, it seemed to come naturally to me. If I'd been career-driven before, being in S Club only reinforced that side of me. The memory of it now makes my head spin, and with hindsight, I think we could have done with a few more holidays. A couple of mini-breaks here and there. Mostly, it was madness, and we seemed to be on the go 24/7 for the five years we were together.

During all this, there were a few interesting and perhaps unexpected moments – the most controversial of which seems quite funny to us all now. '*Spliff Club 7*' was the glaring tabloid headline, and at the time, in 2001, it blew up like some huge scandal.

We were on a busy promotional tour for our single 'Don't Stop Moving' when the now-infamous incident occurred. We were flying high in the charts, and, for some of us, in other ways, too! We were also involved in quite a few campaigns with various brands, including Cadbury – there was a lot happening!

We'd been due to appear on *The Pepsi Chart Show* that day, which was filmed in central London. While us girls were going through the process of getting our hair and make-up done, Brad, Paul and Jon decided to have a little wander around Leicester Square, and at one point they took a turn down one of the alleyways to have a cheeky spliff break. Unbeknown to the boys, they were being watched by an undercover police officer, who'd smelt cannabis as he passed by and then followed them. The officer waited for all three of the boys to take a puff before he swooped in; then they were searched, arrested for possession of drugs, and taken to Charing Cross police station. It must have been scary for them, especially being held in individual cells. In the end, they were cautioned and released without charge, but while all this was happening, it seems someone at the station alerted the press.

After the news reached us at the studio, our performance was pulled and we were all left in a state of shock. This was major, and we all knew it, especially given our clean-cut image. It all felt like such a huge deal at the time, with the story hitting the front page of every tabloid newspaper and beyond. Unsurprisingly, our management went into crisis mode, with phone calls, meetings and general damage limitation.

The day after the story broke, the boys apologised on MTV live, saying how sorry they were. 'We have been very stupid; we know we've made a mistake and we're very sorry,' the statement said.

Always the joker, Jon said to me at the time, 'Oh my God, we've really made it now, we're on the ten o'clock news!' Years later, he told me the scariest thing about the ordeal was the thought of telling his mum. Ironically, we were in the middle of negotiating a brand deal with Sugar Puffs at the time, which sadly did not see the light of day – but it surely could have been an ad exec's dream if you think about it!

We had some hairy moments, too, which, I guess, were all part of being in an incredibly famous pop band with fans and followers of all descriptions. At a record signing in Cologne, Germany, in 2001, the seven of us were all sitting in a row, signing autographs in a store, when we spotted a guy in army fatigues at the back of the room. He didn't exactly look like he was dressed for an S Club 7 record signing, more like a military operation. Still, there were a lot of people there, so at first we didn't take much notice. At one point during the signing, he pointed two fingers in our direction, like he had a gun, and mimed shooting us all, one by one. It was really unnerving, but we carried on with signing and hoped that was the end of it.

When we arrived at the airport to fly home, we spotted the guy again, still dressed in his army gear, in the departure hall. That really did seem a bit too close for comfort, as again, he was staring over at us. This didn't feel like a coincidence; more likely that he'd followed us to the airport, so the best thing we could do was get on the plane and get out of there. Unlike when we were on tour or performing at big events, there was no security with us, just our tour manager.

We went through immigration and security, then got on our flight, but as we settled down in our seats, there he was again. Just sitting there, a few rows along from us, stony-faced. By now, we were all understandably nervous. This man, who'd earlier that day simulated shooting at us, was now on our flight. We were all really scared, knowing that we were about to take off with him on the plane. As the aircraft was filling up with passengers, we decided, along with our tour manager, that we should get off the plane. Like us, she had a bad feeling about this guy, and she didn't want us up in the air with nowhere to run if anything happened. We were all genuinely shaken up as we made our way off the plane. Of course, it was a whole drama, with luggage having to be removed from the hold before the plane could get on its way, but I for one was just happy to be getting off. I have no idea what happened to him or if he posed any real threat, but I'm glad our tour manager did the right thing that day. You just never know.

I'd had another incident a year or so before, when we were all about to climb aboard our tour bus when a guy ran towards us from a crowd of fans and launched himself on me. It all happened so fast, I barely had time to react before the security guards were upon him, dragging him off me and shoving him away. On another occasion, while on tour, a guy burst into our dressing room while we were getting changed. None of us had any idea how he'd got through security or how he knew where to find us, but there he was, standing inches away from me, just staring. Once again, the security team was quick to deal with him. Thankfully, it was as simple and as fast as that, but all of these events were scary at the time.

Being in Asia was always a fantastic experience for us. Our fans in places like Japan, the Philippines and Bangkok made us feel like we were the Beatles. They'd go crazy when we made an appearance, chasing our tour bus and screaming out for us. It was on a different level to other places. There was also the warmth we felt from the fans we got to know well, because they were always there. Often, we'd see the same faces outside the gates of the studios where we'd film *SMTV*, *CD:UK* or *Live & Kicking*. They'd always be there, and we'd sometimes wonder if their parents knew where they were, especially as some of them would camp out all night, waiting for our early-morning arrival at the studios.

As well as the fans, we were so lucky with all the different writers and producers we got to work with: Stephen Lipson, Jewels & Stone (Barry Stone and Julian Gingell), Cathy Dennis, and, of course, Elliot Kennedy and Simon Ellis, to name but a few. We were blessed with having some of the best in the business, who wrote songs both for and with us.

These were busy, crazy times, but as the success of S Club grew and grew, I was still shadowed by insecurity. It wasn't constant, but it was always lurking, ready to jump out at me in a weak moment. It was a quiet unease, a niggling voice – classic imposter syndrome. I sometimes wonder if that ever goes away. I still have it now at times; whenever I do something new, something slightly unknown, there it is. The difference nowadays is that I've found the tools to help me let go of the restrictions I put on myself. I'm learning more about myself every day, and although those things might not all be great epiphanies, they can help me to understand how to sit in my feelings and be comfortable with doing that. For me, it's really empowering.

Chapter 9

MORE MORE MORE

WHEN S CLUB ended, it pretty much just ended. No fanfare or ceremony. We just finished filming at a TV studio one day, performing our final single, 'Say Goodbye', then we all got into cabs and went our separate ways. We didn't even really have much contact once the band ended. It wasn't that we didn't care about one another – we did; there was always love and a special bond. It's just that we were all very different people, and without the glue of S Club, there wasn't any reason to be together. As close as I was to Jo in the band, we didn't even really stay in touch to any great degree. Perhaps that was me, moving on again like I always did – letting things go and not looking back.

So, why did S Club end? Well, I suppose it began with Paul's departure in 2002. I think when someone leaves a big pop band – and it almost always happens – the dynamic changes and it's never the same.

Paul had decided to leave for personal reasons; he wanted to spread his wings. He was very respectful to the rest of us, talking to us and telling us he felt it was the right time, and we, in turn, supported his decision. We even filmed a scene in our TV show *Viva S Club* with Paul leaving, because the show sort of mirrored what was going on in our world. It was sad, of course, but we simply had to respect Paul's decision and move on. Once again, this was something I took in my stride. It was another case of someone who was in my life for a while and then wasn't. I was used to it.

On 3 June 2002, we performed our number-one single, 'Don't Stop Moving' at Party at the Palace, which was held in the gardens of Buckingham Palace as part of the Queen's Golden Jubilee celebrations. This was a memorable one for us in many ways, but particularly because it was our final performance as a '7'. At the end of the song, we said an emotional and public goodbye to Paul, who was leaving the band.

Other acts on the bill that day included Queen, with Brian May playing guitar on the roof of the palace, Annie Lennox, Will Young, Cliff Richard and Sir Paul McCartney. We all performed together at the end of the night, singing 'All You Need Is Love' and 'Hey Jude'. An incredible moment, looking out along the Mall, which seemed like a neverending sea of people all waving Union Jack flags, and knowing that millions of people across the world were watching on TV.

After the performance, we were all invited into Buckingham Palace for a reception. It was quite something, milling around that grand room, with the now King

Charles, Harry and William, and the prime minister of the time, Tony Blair.

After Paul's departure, we released the single 'Alive' from the album *Seeing Double* as 'S Club' – no more 7! We shot the video in LA, and it was a case of business as usual. We missed our friend, but we just had to crack on. After that, we carried on for another year with the release of our movie, *Seeing Double*, and a final single, the aforementioned 'Say Goodbye', which was a double-A side with 'Love Ain't Gonna Wait for You'. At the time, I could have carried on. For some of the others, however, it was a different story. I don't remember any big meeting with Simon or the label to discuss what was going to happen, but there were conversations over time where people voiced opinions about where things were headed. Everyone's take on it will be different, and I don't want to speak for other people, but I knew some of the band found it all-consuming – which it was – and some simply weren't getting what they needed from it, personally. The dynamic of the band had changed, and with all those feelings bubbling to the surface, it just wasn't possible to carry on.

I'd always been career-driven. In fact, my work ethic had been such that I probably would have carried on for a lot longer. S Club had been, in many ways, an escape for me. At the time I was so unaware of myself, I wouldn't have even stopped to ask myself what I needed, as some of the other members of the band might have done. I was go-go-go! I've always been a cup-half-full person, so I always saw the success, which was undeniable and wonderful.

As far as going solo went, there had been no talk of me being the break-out solo performer in S Club before the split. At least, no one had mentioned anything to me. At no point did I go to Simon Fuller and say, 'I want a solo career, can you make it happen, please?' It all just somehow fell into place.

Once the offer was there on the table, I knew I wanted to stay with 19 Management, confident that I had the support and backing of Universal Music and Polydor Records. I also knew I had to grab this opportunity and give it everything I'd got. So there I was, Rachel Stevens, solo artist.

As soon as I heard what was to be my first single, 'Sweet Dreams My LA Ex', I knew it was the song for me. I immediately loved the electro-pop sound of it; it just felt right. This was exactly the direction I wanted to go in; an incredible debut single. My album seemed to be recorded at lightning speed because the music was all there, ready for me to make the decisions I needed to. At that time, in the early 2000s, there were so many teams of great songwriters and producers, all submitting songs for the pop artist of the day. 'Sweet Dreams My LA Ex' was written by Cathy Dennis along with Swedish production team Bloodshy & Avant. Having them on board was exciting for me, because they were producing some amazing cutting-edge pop at the time. Some of the other producers for the album came from the Murlyn production house in Stockholm, who were coming up with some very cool pop music at the time. I was so lucky with the wealth of songs on offer for me, although I wouldn't just record anything that was put in front of me. I knew what I was looking for, and what I liked. Overall, I was very proud of my debut album, but being the contradiction that I am, I was also my worst critic.

The video for 'LA Ex' was extremely slick and cool. It featured me first enclosed in a Perspex box, then entangled in a twisting web of red ribbons among a gang of gorgeous girl dancers. It was the right team and the right choreography at the right time. It did exactly the job we needed it to do, which was to establish me as an artist in my own right. Gone was the more wholesome S Club image, here was the new, sexy, mature Rachel Stevens.

That particular video treatment wasn't the only one we considered, however. There was another treatment from director Baillie Walsh, where I was to perform choreographed movements on a pool towel along with a large and varied group of dancers while sunbathing. That treatment eventually went on to become the video for Kylie Minogue's 'Slow'. They just took out 'Rachel' and added 'Kylie' to the script. Word had it that there were still pages where my name was accidentally left in – 'Rachel moves slowly on a pool towel' when Kylie's team received the script.

The single was released on 15 September 2003, and all week it went back and forth to the number-one spot, going head-to-head with Black Eyed Peas' 'Where Is the Love?' which ended up being the biggest-selling single of the year. Of all the songs to go up against!

On the Sunday of the chart countdown on Radio 1, I threw a garden party at my mum's place, and we all listened excitedly to the top-forty rundown, although I'm sure I knew what number I was going in at by then. As it turned out, 'Sweet Dreams My LA Ex' finally landed at number two, which was a tiny bit disappointing but still a fantastic result. It sold really well, and being up there sandwiched between Black Eyed Peas and Dido's 'White Flag' was pretty epic.

My performance on *Top of the Pops* was incredibly nerve-wracking; there seemed to be so much riding on it. It was my first live performance as a solo artist, and a big deal. We'd had these incredible dancers flown over from Italy by my duo of Italian choreographers, and great styling, hair and make-up on hand. It felt exciting, it felt new, like I was moving forward.

Soon after the release of 'Sweet Dreams My LA Ex', I was invited to perform for Her Majesty The Queen at the Royal Variety Show. What an honour! Having only recently stepped out of the S Club whirlwind, I'd been performing regularly, but at the same time, I knew this would be a huge stand-alone moment, particularly coming so early on in my solo career. Not only was I performing at the iconic London Palladium, but my introduction to the stage was to be delivered by the legend that was Dame Edna Everage – the alter-ego of the late Barry Humphries.

Behind the curtain, nervously waiting to go on, my silhouette of choice was a white waistcoat and flared white trousers, and I was surrounded but eight gorgeous male dancers, all dressed in black (note to self for future engagements – I think they may have helped with my performance). Once I got out there and started singing, I gave it my all, feeling incredibly honoured and proud to be there. Afterwards, I joined the famous line-up to meet the royals, standing next to the lovely Lenny Henry, who, at six foot three, seemed like the tallest man in the world. Before the show, we'd all rehearsed this and had been instructed on what to do when it was our turn to meet the queen. However, even as she approached, I still wasn't quite sure how to greet her. I wanted to be respectful and do it the right way, of course, but being so nervous in anticipation of the moment, I forgot practically everything I'd been told.

Her Majesty was wearing a baby-blue gown, with white gloves, beautiful jewels and a sparkling crown. She looked so elegant and lovely, and as she moved along the line and my turn to meet her drew close, I thought, *Oh my goodness – she's the same height as me!* When we finally said hello, she reminded me of Grandma Pearl: warm, endearing and gracious. I'd loved to have sat down and had a cup of tea with her.

*   *   *

Things were decidedly different for me as a solo artist. As part of S Club, I'd been kept away from much of the decision-making and planning. Now, suddenly, there I was, sitting in boardrooms full of people, who were all focused on me and my career. I'd gone from feeling like I could hide among six other people, to all the attention turning to me – the photoshoots, record sleeves, interviews, videos – all of it. Now, there was no blending into the background if I was having an off day, no letting someone else do the talking. It was all on me.

God, it was intimidating being one of twenty people sitting around a table talking about a music video. In my heart, I knew it was a positive thing, a big step forward in my career, but because it was hard to assert my opinions, the process became scary rather than liberating. I wasn't used to making decisions in that environment and in that way, and didn't feel equipped to do so. And what if I did make a decision or have an opinion? How could I then trust in it? Hearing my voice, even just speaking, sometimes felt uncomfortable. Even after all those years and all my success, the imposter syndrome was still there. It was only later, having gone through therapy and talked to other people, that I realised so many others feel the same at certain points in their life – most people, in fact. Back then, I just saw it as fear and insecurity.

Those feelings of vulnerability often took the shine off what was happening; they masked what creativity was in me.

As a solo artist, looking good in a photograph was always much easier and preferable to giving interviews, because with photographs everything was surface. Deep down, I was still scared of being found out, scared that people might look inside and not like what they found. With photoshoots, I could express myself through physicality, without worrying about how I came across. I particularly liked doing the more sensual shoots. It was a part of me that I nurtured and considered, while other, more important things were forgotten. Shoots with magazines like *FHM* gave me an opportunity to present myself in a different, more grown-up way. It became a form of expression that fitted my persona and I became very adept at playing the role. I was on the cover of about eight issues, which is something I'm still very proud of. That and my 'Rear of the Year' award in 2009 will forever be two of my greatest achievements!

When I first did shoots with *FHM*, I didn't have a clue about their annual '100 Sexiest Women' polls, so I was quite surprised when I first ended up featuring on the list in 2000. *FHM* readers voted in the poll, and after I made the list several more times, it became a big part of my journey. I came second on three occasions; it was very flattering and a lot of fun to be part of. To top it all off, I ended up winning 'Sexiest Woman of All Time' in the poll's twenty-year anniversary list in 2014, just a couple of months after I'd given birth to my second daughter, Minnie. In fact, on my final shoot for the magazine, a few months before that list was published, I was about eight weeks pregnant. Now, it feels like a lovely thing to look back on, knowing Minnie was there with me.

Chapter 10

THE NOUGHTIES

MY FIRST PHOTOSHOOT for *FHM* magazine had been back in 2000, while I was still in the band, and that one featured all four S Club girls. At the time, I hadn't really thought much about it, just that it was fun to be doing a photoshoot for something other than one of the teen mags. As a band, we knew *FHM* wasn't exactly our market, but our management saw the value in us doing it – broadening our appeal, so to speak. Of course, it was all very controlled and completely overseen by our management. There was no way we were suddenly going to do something that might go against the clean-cut image we'd built up over the years, but at the same time, why wouldn't we tap into a new market that was available to us?

Over time, I did *FHM* cover shoots in various locations around the world. For one of the early ones, also while still in the band, Hannah and I travelled to Kenya accompanied by Charl, who was one of the few people I became incredibly close with. She worked for 19 Management on the press side of things. Charl was a big part of my music journey and is still a dear friend to this day.

The internal flight was on one of those tiny planes that I was definitely not a fan of. As we climbed on board, Charl and I spotted a guy on his hands and knees screwing seats into the floor further along the plane. We looked at one another, both knowing what the other was thinking, which was something along the lines of, *Oh God! Get me the hell off this thing!*

'Oh! It's OK, they had to bring an animal on board earlier, so we took the seats out,' somebody helpfully explained.

Right, fine, OK! Deep breaths.

After a bumpy flight, we landed on a small airstrip where we were greeted by people from the Maasai tribe, dressed in brightly coloured robes with beautifully beaded necklaces. They escorted us to the place where we were staying, which was another surprise. The rooms in our accommodation were all open, with no doors or windows, which was quite a culture shock. There were ceilings but not much in the way of walls, just drapes and nets. It was all very lovely, but I wasn't at all comfortable. On top of that, the number of creepy crawlies and insects everywhere was next level. There were creatures I'd never in my life seen before making the most unnerving noises – it really was a far cry from Hampstead.

I felt this weird mix of awe and terror. I knew how fortunate I was to be experiencing this amazing place, but again, wouldn't Sardinia or a Greek island have been better for a photoshoot, not to mention closer to home? I supposed it was all about the amazing landscapes and wild animals, and in those days, the budgets seemed to be bigger. In the end, I don't think I slept a wink, which wasn't ideal the night before a cover shoot.

On the night after the shoot, the Maasai lit a big bonfire and performed the most amazing and energetic tribal dance for us – an explosion of colour, song and music. A moment I will never forget. I'd travelled a fair bit being in S Club, but this was like nothing I'd ever experienced. As daunting as I found some elements of the trip, this was a wild and wonderful pinch-me moment.

Other *FHM* shoots on foreign soil were on slightly more familiar territory. I did shoots in Malibu and central LA, and a fair few in London. Over time, I got to know the creative team at *FHM*, and we worked well together. The shoots were still overseen by 19, and I would be a part of the decision-making regarding the direction they took. What they did to the photographs after they were taken was another matter.

That's the thing I wasn't so keen on, the amount of airbrushing I saw happen in post-production. As much as I enjoyed doing the shoot and the positive reaction that it brought me, I didn't always like the resulting covers because of the way the image could sometimes be manipulated.

It can be quite challenging growing up in the public eye, especially when you're experimenting, changing and growing all the time.

Back then, there were images of me everywhere. Worst of all were the paparazzi photos of what should have been private moments – photos I didn't even know were being taken, with lumps, bumps, tummy out or awkward caught-in-the-moment facial expressions. With all the different shades of lighting and varying camera angles, I sometimes found myself questioning what I actually looked like in real life. Was how I saw myself how others saw me? It brought up a lot of questions, and sometimes still does. Now, there's the added element of ageing, and the availability of social-media filters – Instagram versus reality! It can still sometimes be a challenge to be fully comfortable within my own skin. In so many ways, I feel more comfortable than I ever have, but there are times when I feel insecure, so I'm constantly striving to be the best I can be from the inside out.

As my solo career progressed, my image as a sexy pop princess blossomed, but my feelings of not being good enough only got worse. The resilience of youth had fallen away, and sometimes I felt like I'd been put in a category or a box that I needed to escape from. The irony was that the only person keeping me in that box was me. It became painful. I could see it and I could feel it, but I didn't know how to break free from it.

Deep down, I knew what had to be done. Ultimately, I had to let go of all that tight control. I knew I wasn't being my authentic self, and I knew there was so much more in me than I was giving. When you're constantly trying to micromanage every thought, feeling and event in your life in case something goes wrong, it's exhausting because it's ultimately impossible. That need for everything to be perfect and safe is draining. At some point, it had to stop. It would take years of digging deep and working on myself before that would happen. I certainly didn't come close to breaking free of that control during the heyday of my solo pop career, and I'm sure now I'd have a lot more to say about some of the decisions that were made for me by other people.

Sometimes, I felt like I had to make quick decisions on things that were pretty important, and I agreed to them through fear of missing out or losing an opportunity. At the time, I didn't have the emotional maturity to say, 'Let me have a think and get back to you.' It was something I knew I needed to change and work on, even then. Certain tracks that came my way, for instance. Cathy Dennis wrote 'Can't Get You Out of My Head' for Kylie Minogue and 'Toxic' for Britney Spears, as well as 'Sweet Dreams My LA Ex'. Those songs really could have been snapped up by anyone, because that's the way it worked with writing and production teams back then.

There were some wonderful highs during my solo career. Producer Richard X was so talented and creative, and I loved working with him and Hannah Robinson, who co-wrote my single 'Some Girls'. To me, Richard's music had this amazing Debbie Harry/Blondie-esque vibe. It was cool, edgy pop, and I loved his sound, which felt right for me. 'Some Girls' was released in July 2004 as a charity single for Sports Relief. It was a huge hit, reaching number two in the UK singles chart. The video, directed by Paul Weiland, had me leading an arm-waving parade of young women through the streets of London.

I think, musically, things took a bit of a different direction when I released the single 'Negotiate With Love' from my second album, *Come and Get It*, in 2005. The music industry was morphing and evolving, and although 'Negotiate With Love' was a good song, my instinct was that it wasn't the right direction after 'LA Ex' and 'Some Girls'. I went with the label's decision, but deep down, I felt like it was a departure from the distinct electro-pop sound of those two songs. If I'd followed my instinct and spoken out, I wouldn't have chosen that as a single because I didn't feel as confident about it as I had my other singles. It was hardly a disaster, but it didn't achieve the success of 'Some Girls' and 'LA Ex'. Still, it reached the top ten, and the critical acclaim I received for both my albums was great. In fact, *Come and Get It* appeared on the *Guardian*'s 2007 list of 1,000 albums you must hear before you die.

In June 2004, I performed 'Some Girls' at the Olympic Torch Concert on the Mall in London. It was one of those amazing career high points, with thousands of people gathered in the streets in front of Buckingham Palace and millions watching on TV all over the world. It's a perfect example of what a contradiction I am, and that my life has sometimes been. On the one hand, I've tried to stay protected, private and unseen. On the other, much of my world has been the absolute opposite, including moments like this one when I gave my all doing what I've always loved doing – performing!

From the way I was brought up, to the bullying, then from a career where I was always so very protected and micromanaged. The message I was getting was: stay small, don't get too big for your boots, don't be too anything! While at the same time I was encouraged to be myself, go for it, don't hold back. It's no wonder I felt torn.

In 2005, I was nominated for *Glamour* magazine's Woman of the Year award, which was a really proud moment. The award lunch was held in Berkeley Square Gardens, in London, and although it felt very special to be nominated, I'd need to get up on that stage to accept the award if I somehow won it. The thought of being unscripted in front of an audience was so daunting. I was full of awe and admiration for many of my peers who, to me, seemed so articulate, so natural. I especially admired people who could just be themselves, the ones who could get up there and say, 'Oh my God! I haven't written anything, I'm so bloody nervous!' I love it when people allow themselves to be free and imperfect.

For me, that wasn't an option. I didn't know how at that that point, and as for not having a script, well, that was unthinkable. Before the ceremony, my brain was like jelly. I got dressed and into the car to the venue, then walked the red carpet, where a dozen paparazzi screamed at me to look their way. When the moment came and I was announced as the winner, my hands immediately started shaking. Still, I kept it together, managing a short but sweet thank-you speech, plus I avoided tripping over my gorgeous red gown as I made my way to the stage.

I wonder how I'd feel in a similar situation today. I'd still be nervous, but I realise now that almost everyone getting up and making a speech or accepting an award will have a certain degree of nerves, and that's OK.

Woman of the Year or not, the more successful I became, the more lost I felt. With hindsight, I'm sure I could have gone even further with the opportunities I had if I'd been more present and had more self-belief. I had some great music at my fingertips, I had a good team around me, I was popular – but I struggled to be present and in the moment. The person I am now would have taken control of her career, had the confidence to speak her mind and had more say in creative decisions. Don't get me wrong, I'm extremely proud of what I've achieved, especially given the anxieties that sometimes held me back. Still, I know there were things I let slide at the time that I wouldn't now.

Chapter 11

MATTERS OF
THE HEART

WHEN PEOPLE HAVE interviewed me in the past, I know they've found it hard, and I understand why. My natural instinct sometimes is to stay in my head and protect myself and others. One of the things I find difficult to talk about is my private life, and in particular, my past relationships. Firstly, I get very protective of the person I'm talking about, and secondly, my tendency is to be guarded. What I have come to realise is that I'm speaking from my perspective; making sure I'm always respectful and mindful. So that's been my approach when writing about relationships, too.

My first real public relationship was with actor Jeremy Edwards, who I met through a few mutual friends. We started dating in 2001, through the last year or so of my time in S Club and the beginning of my solo career.

I was very attracted to Jeremy. He was a few years older than me, which I liked, and I thought he would understand the thoughts and feelings I had about living life in the spotlight, given that he was in the same position. With Jeremy, I was still looking for something solid and real. I wanted to feel safe, loved and connected, and I was still grabbing on to situations and to people, whether or not they were right for me. Jeremy and I were not right for one another, and our relationship should have ended a lot sooner than it did. Of course, that's easy to say in hindsight.

Jeremy is a lovely guy who has a lot of great qualities, but our lifestyle choices were polar opposite. Jeremy liked to party hard, while I was a dinner-and-a-glass-of-wine girl. I'm sure there are plenty of couples made up of that same mix of personalities, but long term it's always going to be difficult, as it was with us. Still, as incompatible as we were, I stayed in it. We argued a lot, there was constant drama, and our relationship was difficult and volatile throughout. When you're as vulnerable and lost as I felt back then, you can end up in the sort of co-dependent situation that I found myself in. Whatever it was I was searching for, Jeremy wasn't where I was going to find it.

Still, when he proposed I said yes. It happened with a big romantic gesture – at the Dorchester on Valentine's Day, 2002 – rose petals on the bed, the whole thing. Even as I said the words, agreeing to marry him, I knew it wasn't right. It makes me sad to think of myself being so vulnerable that I said 'yes' to a man who was so clearly not right for me and wasn't going to make me happy. Looking back, though, I totally get it. At the time, there was a big part of me that took comfort in the idea of having love, getting married and potentially making a home. I was overlooking all the glaring problems staring me in the face just to achieve all that. I was clinging on to the romance, to all the good bits – but that wasn't nearly enough to sustain a true and loving relationship. Consequently, I turned away from every red flag, telling myself I could change things and make them better. The worst of it was that our troubled relationship was overflowing into my work and day-to-day life, and I struggled to separate the two.

We never moved in together. Jeremy had a flat in Belsize Park, and I had my flat in Hampstead, but we'd often stay over at one another's places. On one morning – a real early start – I arrived at a video shoot in a very sorry state. Jeremy and I had been up half the night arguing, and consequently I'd had about two hours' sleep. The poor make-up artist had her work cut out. I'm not saying it was all on Jeremy – it takes two to fight – but this was a bad situation that was getting worse. As time went on, the toxicity of our relationship was such that I knew there was no way we could get married; we both knew it wasn't right. Jeremy and I were on completely different paths, which were never going to meet.

When news of our break-up reached the press, it was a story in most of the papers. By that time I'd come to the conclusion that I needed to be on my own and not in a relationship at all. Surely, if I stood on my own two feet and took some time out to be my own person, I'd feel better about myself and my career? As well as that, I'd have no romantic distractions. But alas, that wasn't to be. Not long after breaking up with Jeremy in 2004, I was introduced to a guy called Gavin Dein, a business entrepreneur.

Gavin was a nice guy and I certainly didn't have any of the issues and trauma with him that I'd had with Jeremy. Ultimately, though, Gavin and I weren't right for one another either. If I'm honest, I don't think any romantic relationship would have been right at that time. Still, Gavin was good company, kind and attentive. We had some lovely times together, and we also shared a particularly distressing Christmas together in 2004, experiencing a small after-effect of a huge tragedy.

Both keen to get away from work and take a break, we booked what we thought would be a gorgeous holiday in the Maldives. We were staying in one of those wonderful huts on stilts on a breathtakingly beautiful beach – a gorgeous resort, which looked out over crystal-clear waters. On Boxing Day we woke up to murky, black, choppy waters below us. As well as that, there was debris and luggage floating eerily around. For a while, neither of us could work out what we were seeing. It was as if there'd been some kind of shipwreck and the luggage was washing up on the beach nearby. It turned out that while we'd slept, there'd been a big storm. It hadn't been enough to wake us, but it was enough that the tide had risen, submerging and damaging the jetties that led to our huts, which were now completely cut off from the beach. The luggage we'd seen had been washed out of other guests' beach huts and was now floating in the sea. We didn't realise it at the time, but this was all a repercussion of the earthquake off the west coast of Sumatra and the tragic tsunami that devastated so many communities and coasts in the Indian Ocean. There were no phone lines or internet, and no one knew what was happening. We had to wait for the sea levels to drop before we could go anywhere, and were eventually escorted to the main resort building by hotel staff in life jackets. It was only then that we saw horrendous news of the tsunami on the hotel's big-screen TVs. For safety reasons, we were told that we had to evacuate the island as soon as possible, and as we made plans to leave, we learned more about what had happened. The Maldives had suffered severe damage because of the tsunami, and at least 82 people had been killed there, including a couple of British holidaymakers.

At the time, it was an unnerving experience, but nothing compared to what unfolded on other beaches in the same ocean.

Gavin and I continued dating into the following year, but, as lovely as he was, our relationship was never going to last. Not because it was bad, but because we weren't in love. I was still searching for a deeper connection, despite not knowing what that might be. I realise now that I needed to connect with myself before I could connect with anyone else.

It was a strange and sad time for me. My career was going well and I was successful in my work, but emotionally, I was lost. My confidence was on the floor. I found just enough of what I needed to do my job, but that was as far as it went. The trouble is, when you're constantly searching for what you think might make you happy, you're never actually happy. You're just searching.

Chapter 12

LA BABY!

AFTER MY SECOND album, my record deal came to an end. The industry was changing, but there was no talk of me taking a break or putting things on hold and regrouping. I didn't ask questions or put up a fight when it happened, because I needed a break to work out what I wanted, and, without being dramatic, find out who I was and what might be next for me.

I'd never had to work hard at school because my parents let me coast along, and I'd walked into the London College of Fashion and subsequent jobs without any problem. Ten thousand people auditioned to be in S Club 7, while I was just sitting at the right lunch table. And, when S Club ended, the chance of a solo career seemed to fall into my lap.

Now that had ended, I decided I needed a change and to take control of my life. The idea of living somewhere completely different, where nobody knew 'popstar Rachel Stevens', seemed very appealing. Scary but exciting and necessary. I knew if somebody got chatting with me in a café in California, it probably wouldn't be because they knew who I was, so I decided to go somewhere I was already familiar with and loved: LA.

At the time, Charl was looking after the management side of things for me. She'd left 19, had branched out on her own, and she was still an important and trusted friend. The friend–work relationship can be hard sometimes because the lines can blur slightly, as they did with us on occasion. When you care about somebody as a friend, it can be tricky to sustain a business-like relationship where one works for the other.

Charl saw it all, though. She knew my inner struggles and helped me a lot during that period, including with my plans to be more LA-based. She was there for everything, and I was grateful for such a special relationship.

On my first trip out there while I was finding my feet – in about 2004 – I stayed at Simon Fuller's place in West Hollywood. I met a few people, sorted out a little Mini convertible for myself, flying the British flag, and got used to driving on the huge and busy LA freeways, which wasn't easy. After that, I'd stay out there for three months at a time, just living, chilling out, and even having a few meetings for potential career opportunities in the acting world.

At that point in my life, I didn't know what direction I wanted to go in as far as my career went, which was why I'd gone to LA. I wasn't driven by work at the time, which was a little unnerving for me. I didn't even have an official American agent, just a lovely guy called John Ferriter, who was an agent at Creative Artists Agency (CAA), and who took me under his wing. John took me to a few of the big parties around the Oscars, and I had some acting classes. I'd never really trained in any of the performing arts, so I wanted to see how I'd find it. I even did a handful of auditions – which was a whole other kettle of fish.

Going through the process of auditioning for a role played on every single one of my anxieties and insecurities. I knew if I got a part, I'd throw myself into it wholeheartedly; it was what I had to do to get the role that was the problem. I was so new to it all, and despite all the experience I'd had, I still wasn't prepared for the process of auditioning. I'd been in the business for almost a decade and done so much, including TV and film acting. Still, there I was, walking into these auditions feeling like I'd never in my life worked a single day in the entertainment industry.

I even did some auditions back in the UK, auditioning for the part of Rose Tyler in the 2005 reboot of *Doctor Who*, starring Christopher Eccleston. I was very excited about the role, and got down to the final two, but in the end I lost out to my fellow popstar Billie Piper. It was a great experience, and following on from that, I got my first role in a Hollywood movie – *Deuce Bigalow: European Gigolo*, with Rob Schneider. I mean, blink and you'd miss me, but I was in it nonetheless. The only thing was, when the call came in to 19 Management asking if I'd appear in the movie, there was no mention of the fact that I'd be submerged in a lake and covered in mud – after which I'd emerge from the water all cleaned up and super sexy. I couldn't have felt less sexy if I'd tried when filming the scene. It wasn't my best work, but it was a bit of fun – a tongue-in-cheek cameo in a Hollywood movie. How I never received an Oscar nomination for that appearance is beyond me. I even had my acceptance speech ready!

My original plan for being in LA had been to step away from everything and have time to reset. However, me being me, I couldn't fully commit to not working at all, so I found myself in a kind of no-man's land, where I was still having discussions with John Ferriter while trying to be 'free'. The truth was, I'd lost a lot of my passion and direction for work by that point. I needed to just go and have fun, let loose and explore, which is what I did.

When I wasn't dabbling with work, I was content to live simply in LA. I was happy being on my own, but also enjoying the experience of making some new friends. One evening, I bumped into my London friend Sasha's sister, who was living out there. We started hanging out together, she introduced me to a few more people, and my social circle expanded. By then, I was renting my own place for the duration of my stays and loving my newfound freedom to be me. It was a good time.

I even had a couple of interesting dates while I was there – movie-star dates, in fact! One sunny day while I was hanging out on the beach, I met Stephen Dorff, who was very easy on the eye. I don't even remember how we got talking, but somehow, we did. He asked me out on a date, and I agreed. We went to a lovely Italian restaurant in Malibu, and had a good time. We had a few more dates after that but that's where it ended.

In LA, everything was bigger, flashier and more over the top than it was in the UK. One of the weirdest things I experienced was the gifting suites. As a celebrity, or 'high-profile' person, you're sometimes invited to these big, beautiful houses with amazing grounds and given free things. And when I say things, I mean all sorts – from beauty products to luxury items. Companies give products to celebrities in exchange for them taking a photo with it or wearing it on a red carpet or at a press event. It was such a funny experience, watching people supermarket-sweep the room, while Charl and I were being very British, not wanting to seem blasé and greedy. We watched as various people marched out with an abundance of goodies, not really knowing what to do with ourselves.

I found myself at all sorts of amazing parties with John while I was in LA, and with some big Hollywood stars. Rubbing shoulders with Leonardo DiCaprio at an Oscars after-party is one that springs to mind, and another was somehow ending up at Prince's house in Beverly Hills at a private party. Practically everything in Prince's house was purple; he even had a purple padded lift, which, of course, I couldn't get into because of my claustrophobia. The best part about the night was the incredible, intimate gig that Prince played for his guests – it was beyond amazing to see him perform in that setting. I couldn't believe I was in the same room as someone as iconic and legendary as Prince, let alone his actual house.

I always felt so free and relaxed during my time in LA. I wanted to let go and be spontaneous, to enjoy myself after working so hard for so long and having everything mapped out for me to within an inch of its life. At one point, I took a trip from LA to Las Vegas to meet my mum and Russell, who'd planned a holiday there. We decided to be very 'rock and roll' and get tickets for Barry Manilow, who had a residency at the time. I'd never been to Vegas before, so it was fun to experience the bright lights and crazy energy and, of course, do a spot of shopping.

Over that week, Mum, Russell and I went out for some wonderful meals, experienced the Vegas night life and, as well as seeing Mr Manilow, went to some other shows, including Cirque du Soleil. Barry was the big one, though; he was always one of Mum's favourites. I'd grown up listening to 'Mandy', 'Copacabana' and all his other classics on many a school run with her. Seeing him brought back some lovely memories for both of us.

At the end of one of my stints in LA, I heard about a retreat in Arizona that I thought might be good for me. My therapist at the time had recommended it to me, and being curious about self-development, I decided to take the plunge and book myself in. I wasn't sure what I was expecting, but it wasn't what I ended up with. I was in this place in the middle of the desert, with people who were from all walks of life, from recovering alcoholics to people healing from trauma … and Mike Tyson. I was staying in a chalet on my own in the middle of nowhere, not really connecting to anyone else there. It didn't take me long to realise that this wasn't somewhere I needed to be. This came at a time when I was desperately searching for something; trying to grow and shake off some of the debilitating thoughts and feelings I'd held on to for so long that were holding me back. The focus at the retreat seemed to be on various forms of serious addiction, so it didn't feel like the right fit for me.

Still, I believe there's always something to learn from every experience, and perhaps this was all part of a bigger process. Whatever I was searching for, a retreat in the middle of the desert wasn't where I was going to find it.

Chapter 13

SPARKLES AND CONFETTI

ALEX BOURNE CAME back into my life in 2008 while I was out shopping, not long before my thirtieth birthday. Of course, we'd been girlfriend and boyfriend when we were kids, aged twelve, but on the day that I bumped into him, I hadn't seen him for at least ten years, if not more. At the time, I was at a place in my life where I felt like I should probably be on my own and not in a couple. I was ready to be by myself, excited to be me and to see what the future held, so I was thinking about heading back out to LA for a while to have some fun.

I was in Selfridges, having a mooch and minding my own business, when Alex came over.

'Oh, hi!' he said, looking somewhat surprised.

Alex later told me that as he'd walked into the store that day, he'd had this weird premonition that he'd bump into somebody he knew and that as the thought occurred, I'd suddenly popped into his head.

'Alex, how are you?' I said, just as surprised as he was.

It was nice bumping into him and chatting for a while. He was in a long-term relationship, was acting, and seemed to be doing really well. I filled him in on what was going on with me, and that was all there was to it. After that, we ran into one another a couple more times, once, randomly, at a petrol station, and then a third time in North London, when we eventually swapped numbers and made plans to meet for coffee and a proper catch-up – for old time's sake! It was such an odd thing, not having seen him since I was about eighteen, and then all these chance meetings. It was almost as if it were meant to happen.

When we did sit down over coffee, Alex told me that his relationship wasn't going well, and they were pretty much at the end of the road. Although nothing happened between us until his relationship had ended, it felt good to reconnect. Interestingly, my first thought was that he felt safe – and I mean that in the very best way. Alex was someone I'd had a connection with since childhood. I knew his family, I knew he was a good, trustworthy man. I was still very much looking for that safety, that idea of a close, loving family. He was from the same community in North London with similar morals and values, which also brought a connection.

While I was next in LA, Alex came over so we could spend time together, and it just worked. We shared a love for so many of the same things – food and travel being two of the big ones. We took a wonderful road trip to Santa

Barbara, sampling the local food and visiting wineries. Santa Barbara seemed like a happy place, and that was a happy time.

Things happened pretty fast between us after that. In June 2008, almost a year after we'd got together, we took a trip to Ostuni, in Puglia, which is a beautiful town with clusters of white-washed houses that sit on a hillside beneath a stunning Gothic cathedral. The town is full of winding back streets, passages and lots of steps, and it's a great place to wander and get lost. While we were there, we stayed at his friend's trullo, which is a traditional stone house specific to that area of southern Italy.

We were at a lovely restaurant in the town one night, and I was slightly baffled as to why Alex was carrying this huge bag with him.

'What's in that bag? Why have you got that big bag?' I asked, to which he smiled and said nothing.

Little did I know, he was hiding an engagement ring inside the giant bag, and at one point in the evening, he pulled out the ring and asked me to marry him. It was something I hadn't seen coming. In fact, I was quite taken aback. We'd done so much since getting back together, but still, this felt a bit fast. I wasn't even sure I was ready for it. It feels strange putting this down on paper now, uncomfortable even, but that was the truth of it. That's not to say I didn't think he was the man I was going to be with, it just all happened so fast. I was also certain that he would be the man I'd marry because I loved him. I just don't think I was quite ready when he asked me.

As I've said, I'm someone who loves love. I'm passionate about true love and it was something I'd been searching for my whole life. Of course, I said a big 'yes', but at the same time, deep down, I knew I needed to be sure I'd said it because I'd finally found that deep connection, not just because it would give me all the things I wanted and thought I needed – a home, a family and children.

Not long after Alex's proposal, I got a call from Charl asking if I'd be interested in taking part in *Strictly Come Dancing* later that year. It was the show's sixth series, so relatively early days given that it's now past series twenty-one! Back then, I hadn't really watched the show and didn't know much about it. Still, I loved dancing and learning new skills, and it wasn't as if I was drowning in opportunities for work at that time either. In fact, I didn't really know where my career was going, so I knew I should grab the chance while it was there.

Shows like *Strictly, Dancing on Ice* or *MasterChef* – all of which I've taken part in over the years – are such great opportunities to step outside yourself and do something fresh and different, something that challenges you and teaches you something new. As a performer, it also opens new doors, especially with a show as big and high-profile as

Strictly. Being on live TV every Saturday night, plus doing all the press and TV sofa chats, meant I would be firmly back in the public eye. My vulnerability when stepping outside my comfort zone, and having been out of the spotlight for some time, meant this new venture might be challenging, but I knew I had to go for it. This was an opportunity I couldn't turn down.

My partner on *Strictly* was Vincent Simone, the Italian professional who was born into a family of dancers. In fact, both his parents were Latin and ballroom dancers. Vincent was a sweetheart and I adored him, but he was always in character – Vincent, the Italian lothario – so he was a bit hard to get to know on a deeper level. We got on like a house on fire, but I'd have liked to see more of the man behind the alter-ego, and had more of a personal working relationship with him rather than just all for show. Perhaps I recognised this trait in Vincent because it's so often what I'd done myself, hidden behind a professional mask rather than showing my true self.

We did have fun, though, and Vincent was an incredibly talented dancer and a joy to be with during training, which was hard work. Being on camera the whole time was a challenge, and have I mentioned that I'm not good at getting things wrong and making mistakes? As usual, I was the perfectionist, striving to get everything right. This can sometimes take away the fun, creative element of what I'm doing, which, in many ways, is just as important as the competitive aspect – perhaps even more so. When I look back on it now, I realise that nobody cares if you make a mistake, and it's OK to mess up. At the time, however, all those tricky elements piled on extra pressure, and that was on top of all the usual nerves that come with a live TV show – especially when it's the most-watched show on TV every week. I know I'd handle it much better now, but having a camera in my face the whole time – having to be me – really played into all my insecurities.

Of course, the show's producers were keen to capture our emotions, our highs and lows, during the competition, but the last thing I felt comfortable with was being vulnerable in front of the cameras. The idea of letting my hair down and showing the real me was alien, and it showed. The comment I got most from the judging panel usually started with something like, 'If you just let yourself go, Rachel …'

I knew they were right, because although I was enjoying myself, I was always holding something back, just in case I gave my all and then failed.

During the series, it often seemed like there was an expectation that I would be good or that I had an advantage, having come from a pop background where I'd done a fair bit of choreography. Of course, anyone who's been to drama or dance school, or who's been in a pop band, is going to have had training to varying degrees, but the dancing I'd done in S Club and beyond was a world away from what was expected here. Ballroom dancing is so incredibly precise, so beautifully synchronised. I'd never done anything like it.

It was a nice surprise, then, to a receive a compliment from someone rather special when I attended an event for Help for Heroes – a charity which supports members of the British Armed Forces with their physical and mental health, among other things. While I was at the event, Camilla Parker Bowles (or Queen Camilla as she now is) approached me.

'You're amazing,' she said. 'I've been voting for you every week.'

It was such a lovely, generous thing to say and it meant a lot to me.

As with any competition show where the public has a say, *Strictly* is as much a popularity contest as anything. As with all TV reality shows, there's a bit of manipulation of stories involved to bring out the characters of the contestants and an agenda for each one. Everyone had a role to play, and that's to be expected. It's television, and there has to be a behind-the-scenes backstory to make those Saturday-night performances feel even more crucial and dramatic.

Strictly was a full-on schedule every week. As well as learning the dance, we had our VTs and behind-the-scenes stuff to film, and promotion to do. It got to the stage where I would actually dream the dance steps, as if I were still learning and performing the routines as I slept; the training was that intense. There was no time for Christmas shopping or preparations for the holiday that year either. As well as the main show and the results show, there was also the companion show, *Strictly Come Dancing: It Takes Two*, to film interviews and segments for.

After a couple of weeks, as I got more into the show, I started to get so much more involved with my styling and costumes, working with the show's incredible design team whenever I could. Once I got going with that, of course, there was no stopping me. The wardrobe people were thrilled that I was so enthusiastic. I knew what suited me, what worked and what didn't, and it was fun being part of that process, seeing all the beautiful costumes come to life.

Some of my fellow contestants on the series were Jodie Kidd, Phil Daniels, Lisa Snowdon, Heather Small and political correspondent John Sergeant. John ended up leaving the competition because week on week the public kept voting him in, despite him not being the greatest dancer, and eventually he was worried he might actually win.

Everyone was friendly and professional, and there was such a varied mix of characters on the show. Jodie Kidd was so lovely; I have a hilarious picture of the two of us, with Jodie, at over six foot, towering above me.

As the series went on, you couldn't help but get swept up in the emotion and drama of it all. As far as the dances went, I found myself loving the really intense, passionate and sensual ones the most – the tango and the rumba – and I got my highest scores in those dances. Every week during the vote-off, my heart would be in my mouth until our names were called out. The few times I found myself in the bottom two were just horrible. A part of me couldn't help but take it to heart, it was impossible not to. I knew it was all part of the process and I knew how TV worked – it's not serious; it's sometimes almost panto and I got that – but in shows like *Strictly*, you put everything into it. I cared so much about doing my best that finding myself in that position was upsetting.

In the end, I came second to actor Tom Chambers, although I would have loved to come first. For me, it wasn't about being better than other contestants, it was about being the best I could be and wanting everyone to do well. For a long time, I had the record for getting the most tens in one series, so I'll take that!

After the series ended, I went straight on to do the *Strictly Live!* tour in January, and it was fun to get out there and dance again, as well as see everyone. Plus, I finally got my hands on that glitter ball! I also took part in a couple of Christmas specials. I even did another tour much later down the line, in 2015, when I got a call out of the blue to ask me if I would fill in for someone who had to pull out, so that was a nice little surprise.

All in all, doing *Strictly* was a huge, full-on experience; I'm pretty sure both Alex and Nikki had PTSD for a good couple of years after that show ended; triggered every time they heard the opening theme music. It came at a time when

I was looking for a new direction, career wise, unsure of what I wanted or needed. I was suddenly back out there on primetime TV and in the public consciousness, but *Strictly* was just a big, bright sparkly burst rather than an ongoing new direction. Surely, there had to be more.

Chapter 14

THE ATTACK

JUST BEFORE OUR engagement, Alex and I had decided to live together, which was an exciting and lovely next step. We moved into a cosy lower-ground-floor flat in Primrose Hill – a special part of London I'd long been in love with. We made the place our own, with the help of an incredibly talented and eccentric interior designer called Sera of London. This very quickly became another creative outlet for me and I started to develop a real passion for interior design. From choosing elegant wallpaper and pretty lamps to quirky or fun pieces of art, I loved working alongside such a bright and creative energy. It was a happy and meaningful time making a home, but unbeknown to me, there was a traumatic event on the horizon.

It happened a few months after I'd finished *Strictly*. It was June 2009, outside what was then our relatively new flat, and I'd just arrived home after doing a supermarket shop. Getting out of the car with a few bags of shopping, I headed down the path, then walked through the front door into the tiny hallway from where the stairs led down to our flat. As

I turned to close the front door, hands full of shopping bags, I saw a guy charging along the path towards me. For a split second, I thought, *Oh, it must be someone I know*, but suddenly he was throwing himself at me, knocking me backwards. I hardly had time to breathe as we tumbled to the bottom of the stairs, let alone think. The shopping flew everywhere, and the man, wearing a balaclava, was now on top of me with his hand around my neck.

'If you scream, I'll fucking break your neck.'

His aggression was terrifying and sent a rush of pure fear through me. I was more terrified than I'd been in my entire life, but then something else kicked in – the need to survive.

Don't fight! Just give him what he wants.

It all happened so fast. Before I could think what to do next, he was ripping my earrings out of my ears, stripping me of every piece of jewellery I was wearing – engagement ring, diamond necklace, Rolex watch. Not that I cared about any of that; I literally went into survival mode at that point.

While we were on the floor, I became aware of other bodies moving above us. Two more men, who rushed past us into the flat and helped themselves to my computer, more jewellery and anything else of value they could carry. They weren't in the flat long. Before I could move or even think, the three of them were out of there and fleeing the scene. I dragged myself off the floor and stumbled upstairs, my instinct telling me to get out of the flat and into the open air.

I called Alex to tell him what had happened, and then my brothers, who came over immediately. They ended up going out in a car looking for the men, furiously angry. My brothers are two soft and beautiful souls, but don't mess with them!

Once I'd called the police and Alex was home, I said a little prayer of thanks that nothing worse or more violent had happened. Yes, I was pretty battered and bruised, but it could have been so much worse. Over the years, I've tried not to replay it in my head, but on occasions, I've experienced flashbacks, which send shivers down my spine. I was a woman alone with three men who'd attacked me in my home – somewhere I'd thought of as my safe place. Our flat never felt the same to me after that.

The police did apprehend some suspects and, a week or so later, I had to attend a police line-up. I thought I recognised one of the men in the line-up, but I couldn't be 100 per cent sure it was him. The guy had been wearing a balaclava when he attacked me, and it was all so fast and blurry. I couldn't commit or say for certain. Thankfully, though, my attackers were caught. It turned out to be a gang that had targeted several other well-known or high-profile people in St John's Wood, Hampstead and Primrose Hill.

The ordeal may have been over and the offenders convicted, but there were after-effects. The PTSD I suffered after the attack was terrible. I couldn't even leave the house for a while. For the next couple of weeks, Alex would leave for work each morning and, at my request, lock me in the flat, but even then, I didn't feel safe. I wouldn't open the door to anyone, always checking who might be lurking outside. If did spot any men in a vehicle, it would send me into a panic. If I did go out, I'd sometimes have to sit in my car when I got home until I felt safe enough to go inside.

Unfortunately, that wasn't the end to the trauma. What happened next, just a few weeks later, was like something out of a movie. I was in Harry Morgan – the Jewish restaurant and North London institution – with my mum and Russell, Alex and his parents. It was a Friday evening, and I was there eating chicken soup and chatting away, when a man rushed through the door into the takeaway section of the restaurant – separated from us by a wall and a doorway. I remember hearing what I thought were party poppers going off, but then a man wearing a motorbike helmet ran into the dining area, waving a gun. We all instinctively jumped up as the man started spraying bullets, and before I knew it, I was under the table, with my mum throwing herself on top of me. With St John's Wood being a fairly affluent area, I assumed, in my panic, that this was another robbery.

Within a few seconds, it was all over. The shooting stopped, the man had gone, and we slowly emerged from hiding to find broken glass and furniture everywhere. It turned out to be another gang-related incident.

After these two events, I was scared all the time. I was scared just coming out of my front door and getting out of my car. There were times when I sat in my car unable to move simply because there was someone sitting in the car in front of me. I'd sit there, frozen with fear, slowly but surely convincing myself that this innocent person was there to jump out and attack me the second I opened the car door and stepped out. Even now, if someone knocks at my front door and I'm not expecting anyone, I get really jumpy. My heart leaps into my mouth, and my mind goes into a spin.

Chapter 15

MARRIAGE AND MOTHERHOOD

THE TIME HAD come to start planning our big day. We were both so excited and couldn't wait to get started. When it came to planning, I realised quite quickly that Alex and I had very different skills sets and approached organisation in very different ways. This sometimes resulted in things becoming more stressful that they needed to be. We both got quite emotional at times, simply because we cared so much about every detail, and wanted our special day to be the best it could be. What I realised from this was that Alex was a doer, and if he's got something to achieve he really goes for it.

Meanwhile, in the lead-up to our big day, not long having come out of the *Strictly* bubble, some of the things left to me to organise ended up being a bit last minute. Fortunately, no decisions were made without both of us agreeing except, of course, about the dresses.

Our original plan had been to get married in France – somewhere incredibly romantic and picturesque. When we got the quote for the costs, however, it was a case of, 'Do you know what? London would be really great!' Not that we did it on a budget. We ended up having our wedding at Claridge's, which felt right for us – very beautiful, very London. Our wedding ended up being covered by *OK!* and we got to share some gorgeous photos in the magazine, which was a special keepsake.

My dress was designed by an Israeli designer called Mira Zwillinger. Having her gorgeous creation fitted and made bespoke for me was very special. I flew out to Israel to work on it with Mira, and for that, I had Mum by my side; it was such a lovely experience for us to share.

On the wedding day itself, Mum was so nervous and anxious that I felt like I needed to comfort her rather than the other way around. My niece Ella, Jason's daughter, was our bridesmaid, and my nephew Bailey, Leigh's son, was our page boy, and my goodness they looked cute.

Sadly, my dad wasn't at my wedding, as he wasn't in my life at that time. We've had a complicated journey, he and I, and for a long time, my relationship with him was distant. At the time of the wedding, rebuilding at that point wasn't an option; I know I had a lot of healing to do first. Later, in 2011, I did reach out to him, when I was emotionally ready. I went into it without expectations. I wasn't expecting any acknowledgement of what had happened, an apology or any great outpouring of emotion. I was just ready to reach out and reconnect in whatever form that took. I realised that, like us all, parents can be flawed humans. Although the pain never completely goes away, I was ready to grow from it, and learn to let go of that pain.

Our wedding ceremony was a traditional Jewish one. Alex and I said our vows under the chuppah, which was beautiful, and did the breaking of the glass, all under the watchful gaze of a well-known Jewish wedding planner who helped us organise everything. I've always thought it was important to make a wedding day uniquely personal, and although we did that with our reception, looking back, the ceremony was slightly too religious for me. We had a rabbi who sang the whole ceremony in Hebrew, and it was heavy on faith. I love being Jewish, but the things I love are the importance placed on family, community and traditions, like Friday-night dinner for example. For me, being Jewish is about the principles rather than the religion. I take from the religion the ideals that mean something to me.

As for the party – well, now we're talking! We really felt the love in that room, surrounded by about two hundred of our family and dear friends, including, of course, Grandma Pearl, being the amazing, glamorous woman that she always was. There's a wonderful shot of her, smiling happily, in one of my videos from the day, when Alex and I were standing under the chuppah.

Alex and I are both massive foodies, so that was right up there on the priority list (in fact, the food tasting might have been my favourite part of the entire planning process). We had the most fabulous musicians play for all our guests, thanks to musical director Joseph Ross, who's one of the brilliant musicians that toured with S Club back in the day. Also, *Strictly Come Dancing* professionals Ola and James Jordan performed some spectacular dances. There were plenty of other special and moving moments throughout the night, too.

Once the excitement of the wedding was over, Alex and I settled into our new life. I wasn't sure what I was going to do next career-wise, and Alex had also been going through changes on the work front. As a child, Alex had a performing background, going to drama school and being part of the National Youth Music Theatre, and coincidentally had crossed paths with Hannah and Paul. Then, as an actor, he was in some adverts, TV shows and theatre. I think there were elements of the industry that he would say he struggled with, as I did. Now we were married, financial security was his priority and he started looking for a new path to tread. After taking the time and focusing on a new direction, Alex found his calling – in property. He worked hard, built up his business over time, and now owns his own high-end property company based in central London.

Although we both knew we really wanted to start a family, we'd only just had the discussion about it when I first got pregnant. In fact, it was a complete surprise. The most wonderful surprise! Of course, it happened when it was supposed to happen, but at the time, I probably would have taken it more slowly.

On the morning I found myself alone in our flat, looking down at a positive pregnancy test, I called Alex in a state of shock, just to find out what time he'd be home. As it turned out, he was running late that night, but this wasn't something I wanted to tell him over the phone. It was the last thing I was expecting and I felt every emotion – surprise, joy, nervousness, excitement – all at once. As soon as Alex walked in the door that evening, I showed him the test.

'I'm pregnant,' I announced, still not quite believing it myself.

'Really? Are you sure?'

'Well, we can do another test, but this one says I am.'

We did a second test, which confirmed I was indeed pregnant, and then it was just pure joy. We were both over the moon and so excited. Once it had sunk in, we called Mum and Russell to tell them the happy news, then drove around to Alex's parents' place to tell them. Everyone was overjoyed at the thought of a new member of the family; it was such an exciting time.

I was very fortunate throughout my pregnancy. Apart from feeling nauseous for the first four months, it all went pretty smoothly. The problem with the nausea was that my old phobia of being sick came into play in a big way. It certainly wasn't as prevalent as it had been in the past, when I'd have full-blown panic attacks and get in a real state about it, but it did make going out and about tricky. Even now it's really triggering; if I hear that one of the kids at school has been sick, or I feel unwell, it sends me into a head spin. I'm just a bit better at dealing with it these days. I think what helped me when I was carrying Amelie was the knowledge that my body was doing something amazing. *I* was doing something amazing.

As for work, I did bits and bobs, but I wasn't working on any big projects. I think being pregnant gave me a new purpose, an incredibly special one, so all I wanted to do was nest and prepare for the arrival of our child. The only pressure I put on myself was knowing when to stop and restart my work life, because there is no such thing as maternity leave in the entertainment industry, so it's difficult to navigate.

After working with Charl, I went to a company called Finch + Partners, who had an amazing roster of high-profile people in fashion, entertainment, sport and art, connecting them with big brands for endorsement deals. I went to a few fancy parties, polo matches and a few auditions, but it was a different world than I was used to at that point, so my partnership with Finch + Partners didn't come to much, and I remained at a bit of a loose end.

One of the other things I found particularly hard, coming out of the world of work, was not having a diary fully prepared for me by a management team. I missed the structure and being part of a team, but I especially missed being creative, having a focus and direction. Schedules were no longer prepared for us and there were no cars to take us to wherever we needed to go and there was nowhere I needed to be. When you come out of that world after so many years, it's ingrained in you, and it can be hard to adapt to another way.

Over time, I've learned how important it is for me to have structure and consistency in my day – I think we all need that to some degree – so I took it upon myself to work at being a lady who lunched while I was pregnant, making sure my unborn child was well fed.

Thinking about a particular lunch with Nikki, I recall having a 'Physic Sally' moment when I was about four months pregnant. At the time, all my senses were heightened, and for some strange reason I knew, just by looking at her, that something about her was different.

'Are you pregnant, Nikki?' I asked her, quickly followed by, 'Oh my god! I shouldn't have asked that!'

Being pregnant is one of those things you can't lie about between friends – especially friends who are always honest with one another, as we are. But at the same time, you only want to tell when you're ready to tell. Still, there was a knowing twinkle in Nikki's eye across the table.

'I am,' she smiled. 'By just a couple of weeks.'

'I knew it!'

My best friend and I were pregnant at the same time. We'd grown up together, got married around the same time, and now we were both having our first child. It didn't get any better than that.

Another sense that was in full effect during pregnancy was my sense of smell. It was so heightened that I couldn't even step into a supermarket for feeling nauseous with the wall of various aromas that hit me. Also, as a proud tea connoisseur and lover, I couldn't believe that I couldn't drink my beloved Yorkshire Gold until after the baby was born (or any tea or coffee) because I couldn't bear the taste or even the smell of it. That was a tough one but, of course, worth the wait.

Once I made it past the sickness bit of my pregnancy, I really started to enjoy the experience. I loved nesting, getting organised and planning; it was a warm, wonderful time, and, boy, did I love making a list. (I still do.) I had a great obstetrician and NCT antenatal support, and when it came to the birth, it was all very straightforward and relaxed. Going into labour was so exciting. The contractions began, but very mildly, so we took ourselves for a walk in Regent's Park, where Alex stopped for a hot dog while counting down the minutes between contractions.

We had a playlist of music planned and had a well-organised schedule, but I'd kept it in mind that I should remain open to change and things not going to plan. I was determined to let nature take its course and just go with it, which, given my usual anxiety, was pretty good for me. The only time I felt vulnerable in the lead-up to the birth was when I had the epidural – having an injection into my spine while staying perfectly still mid-contraction was pretty scary. Apart from that, it was all pretty dreamy, and I felt very well looked after. Everyone looks out for you when you're having your first baby – as well as Alex, who was amazing and a real support throughout my labour, the nurses, doctors and my friends were all super-attentive. Once you get to the second child, however, it's a different story. You've already got a toddler climbing all over you, so you just have to get on with it.

There was one slightly hairy moment after Amelie was born. Only seconds after, there were alarms going off all around me because I'd lost so much blood. Suddenly, there were people rushing into the room on high alert. It was all-hands on deck while I was lying there, not knowing what was going on. Thankfully, the doctors quickly got everything under control, and in the end everything was fine.

It was after the birth that I really struggled. Like many first-time parents, I found motherhood difficult. I was acutely aware that in the space of a single day, my life had changed forever, and as the days went on, the realisation that I was responsible for this beautiful little human was overwhelming me. I wondered if all new parents felt the same, or was it just me? One of the things I learned very quickly was that once you've had a child, sleep will never be the same. As every woman knows, the physicality of giving birth is exhausting, and then there's this little person who needs attention and feeding at all times of the day or night.

After a few weeks, Alex went back to work, and there was a little part of me, left alone as a new mum, that was envious of that. Alex had structure and, I felt, more freedom. For me, so much had changed, and it was hard for me to accept and get used to. On top of all of that, the PTSD from the attack at our flat was still with me, but now it wasn't just myself I needed to protect, I also had this little person to keep safe. I don't think anyone quite realised how deep this all went with me, but I understand why. I was keeping it all inside, trying to focus on being the best new mum I could be.

Alex and I loved one another, but I found it very difficult to reach out, ask for help, and share my insecurities and vulnerabilities in this new phase of our life. Consequently, I was ill-equipped to ask for what I needed from Alex and let him in, and that was isolating for both of us. It was a similar situation with my mum. As wonderful as she is, she wasn't naturally hands-on with helping out, and there were times when I could have done with that. Once again, I didn't know how to ask her, despite knowing that she's always there when I need her. Not knowing how to speak up and ask for what I need has been a challenge, and, in the end, I did what I always did and just got on with it.

Once again during that time, it was Nikki who was by my side. She'd also just had her daughter, Leah, and she and

I were now one another's support group. We'd take our girls for long walks, put the world to rights and compare notes, reminding one another how well we were doing, and what brilliant mums we were striving to be.

Chapter 16

FAMILY LIFE

ALEX AND I planned for Minnie, our second baby. After Amelie was born in 2010, I knew I wanted a second child, and once again, thankfully, I fell pregnant quite easily. I knew how fortunate I was with that, and I was grateful.

At first when I took a pregnancy test it was negative, but that turned out to be wrong. By the time I took another and found out I was pregnant after all, I was actually much further along than I thought. With Amelie, I hadn't found out her sex before she was born, but with Minnie, we did, and I was overjoyed to be having another girl. Once again, it was a pretty smooth pregnancy, and this time, I gave birth at the Lindo Wing, St Mary's Hospital. Again, the medical team were exceptionally supportive and it was a beautiful experience.

Our little Minnie has since grown into a gorgeous ten-year-old and, in many ways, she is the more resilient of our two kids. She's very logical in her thinking and wiser than her years. If I've forgotten something, Minnie is always the one to pick me up on it or remind me, and she always knows exactly what she wants.

Amelie was singing in tune by the time she was five; she lives and breathes singing and performing, and I know that as she carries on blossoming she will always have a passion for creativity. In fact, she's already started her career, appearing in the West End in *Les Misérables* for a year as a young Eponine and then later a young Coisette when she was just ten.

Minnie also loves performing, but I think for a long time she held back, thinking that performing was Amelie's thing. Recently, though, she's been coming out of herself, and she's quite the sass-pot. Minnie is also very academic, so hopefully many opportunities lie ahead of her, and I will strive to support them both in their passions and things they want to pursue. The best thing we can do for our children is to give them opportunities and encourage them to grow into the people they want to be, to steer them towards good choices, but ultimately let them find their own path, too.

As I write this, I'm preparing for Amelie's Bat Mitzvah, which is the ceremony or event that denotes a young woman becoming an adult in Jewish law. Although I don't observe all the religious traditions in the faith, I was happy for Amelie to have a Bat Mitzvah as long as she understood why she was having it. She had to put the work in but also make it personal to her. She's not going the whole way with it, and her event isn't going to be held at a synagogue, but she will recite the Shema, which is a Jewish holy prayer, and

Meeting HRH Queen Elizabeth II, 2003.

In the studio recording Band Aid, 2004.

With Emma Bunton and Jamie Cullum.

Glamour Woman of the Year! 2005.

With my mum and Russell on our trip to Vegas, 2008.

Performing on *Strictly* with my dance
partner Vincent Simone, 2008.

A mother–daughter dance on
my wedding day, 2009.

A shot from my 2010 calendar.

My gorgeous girls,
Amelie and Minnie, 2018.

Conferring with my fellow judge on *The Voice*, 2015.

Heading on stage at
Proud Cabaret, 2020.

One of my go-to looks:
minimal and classic, 2021.

With Mum and my brothers, Leigh and Jason.

A life-changing moment – meeting Brendyn on *Dancing on Ice*, 2022.

Smiling through the nerves for
a live performance.

On a shoot nursing my
broken wrist.

Adding radio DJ to my CV!

Back with the S Club girls at
the BRITs, 2023.

Me and Nikki, still smiling!

With Nikki and our families at the S Club reunion.

More backstage support
from Nikki.

S Club: the 2023 edition.

Warming up for the show.

Back doing what I love best!

she's learning the significance behind the tradition of Bat Mitzvah.

As Alex and I continued our journey of parenthood together, we formed such special and close relationships with our girls, but as a couple, we had our ups and downs. As time went on, the children grew, life became even busier, and it felt more and more like Alex and I were speaking different languages. We both had things to say, but neither of us could hear or understand what the other was saying.

Alex and I both loved a tidy home, but when you're doing school runs, bath times, work and everything else, I felt pressure to keep on top of everything. In my line of work, I couldn't plan a structured week-by-week diary. If a job came up for me the following day, I'd have to work, juggle the school run, my appointments and other commitments, as many parents do. I found that hard. While I absolutely adore our girls – they are always my number-one priority – I did struggle with trying to keep my career going while trying to be a mum and a wife, and make a home. My need for a creative outlet was still very strong, and sometimes that part of me was getting lost. I really struggled with that.

Alex was extremely supportive of my career, but if I had work one day and one of our kids was ill, I would have to adapt accordingly while Alex's schedule was very structured. For me, this conflicting dynamic put a strain on our relationship. We were pulling in different directions rather than coming together. The differences between us became clearer and eventually made us grow apart.

I felt lonely in our marriage, and I realise now that part of that was me emotionally isolating myself. I'm not a stay-at-home mum, and I never could be. My career was always important to me, but I struggled with feelings of guilt and feeling like I wasn't good enough.

It was heartbreaking and hard to navigate, especially with the children being at the forefront of my mind. The last thing I wanted was for them to get hurt in the process of our break-up, as I had been, but in my heart, I worried that was where we were heading.

We'd recently moved to a new house just as Covid hit, and, like most people, I was very scared at the start of it all. Those initial news stories about a new virus that was killing people were terrifying, and my biggest worry was for all our loved ones. With the closing of schools and adjusting to the new normal, I felt bombarded as a parent.

'Home-schooling! This is what you need to do, this is how you need to do it!'

I remember thinking, *Hang on, can we just get our heads around what's happening in the world and just be for a minute?* I found it tough taking on the role of teacher to my children.

Meanwhile, the girls were anxious about what was going on all around them. We were more concerned with their mental health than them needing to finish their times tables. Of course, I didn't want them falling behind, but they were six and nine – there was time to catch up and get back on track. What was most important to me was that we were talking and listening to one another.

The upside of lockdown was that there seemed to be a wealth of creativity and wonderful projects popping up online and on social media. One of my lockdown highlights was doing Gary Barlow's Crooner Sessions, where he hooked up online with various pop stars and artists and performed a duet of one of the guest artists' most famous songs. Being a fan of Gary's, I'd watched a couple and really enjoyed them, and then, out of the blue, I got an email from the man himself, asking if I fancied coming on. For my Crooner Session, we performed 'Sweet Dreams My LA Ex', and had such a lot of fun. I was honoured and excited to be a part of it, especially having the gorgeous Gary Barlow singing one of my songs with me – such an epic moment.

One of the things that kept me laughing was my Covid meet-ups with Nikki. Priceless moments when we laughed, cried and went through every emotion in between. When I look back on that time now, it feels crazy to think that we'd be out in a park or on one another's doorstep, trying to keep our kids – who are like mini versions of the two of us

– apart. We were doing what best friends do, helping each other through a tough time, just by being there.

Also, in contrast to all the difficult stuff happening between us, Alex and I managed to carve out some wonderful times during the pandemic. In the beautiful summer of that first lockdown, we went on some lovely family walks, ordered Mindful Chef recipe boxes and spent time together as a family.

Those moments were precious – good things coming from a bad situation. Sadly, it wasn't enough to stop what was eventually to come.

Chapter 17

GIVING BACK

THROUGHOUT MY CAREER, I've had lots of opportunities to work with various charities, all of which have been inspiring and incredibly rewarding. One of the most memorable trips I made in conjunction with a charity was in 2013 for WaterAid. They provide clean water and hygienic toilet systems to communities who need them. The trip came about after I met a woman who worked for WaterAid at an event, and we got talking. It blew my mind to learn how many communities around the world don't have clean drinking water – something we all take for granted and see as a basic human right. So, when WaterAid approached me to travel to Africa to highlight some of the work they were doing, I was curious to learn more and find out how I might get involved.

When people don't have a reliable source of clean water, they have no choice but to use dirty water for drinking and cooking, which spreads disease, and much of the time they have to walk miles to collect that dirty water. My trip – with Charl and a documentary film crew – was to look at communities before and after WaterAid had come in and installed water supplies. As was usual when doing something outside my comfort zone, I was nervous about the unknown, wondering what to expect and what was expected of me. One half of my brain was telling me how incredible it was to have the opportunity to do this, while the other half was spinning with thoughts and insecurities.

For the trip, we flew into Addis Ababa in Ethiopia before making a three-hour trip by Jeep over dusty dirt roads to the Jeldu region. The drive was quite something. Driving across the plains, I was surprised at how beautifully green and lush everything was.

Word had got around that we were coming, and many locals followed us along the road as we neared our destination. As we drove into the village, a mass of people headed towards us. As they got nearer, I realised they were children, all running towards us with curiosity. It was a wonderful and warm welcome, and a breathtaking sight to witness. I was quite emotional.

Although I'd had a few prep talks with people from the charity beforehand, nothing could have prepared me for some of the things I experienced while I was there. It was all very well hearing about the plight of people there, but it's impossible to imagine the magnitude of it until you see it.

When I got out of the car at our village destination, I said hello to as many of the children as I could. One little boy walked over to where Charl was standing, so she took his photograph. The boy had never seen a camera before, let alone a phone, so when Charl turned the camera around to show the boy his own image, he was gobsmacked and delighted. After that, a queue formed with all the kids wanting to have the experience of seeing their picture.

From there, we were taken to a small brown house that was little more than a hut. There I met a widowed mother, who was around my age, with her eight children. The walls and floor of their house were mud, but she had dressed in her best clothes in anticipation of our visit, which was immediately moving. As I sat down to speak to her, I held her hand and listened to what she had to say about the community's struggles with having no nearby clean water.

Because the region we were in was so remote, we needed two interpreters instead of just one. There are over 80 languages spoken in Ethiopia, so one person translated from English to a more widely used Ethiopian language, then the second translated it into the more regional dialect that the lady spoke. Then, it had to come through two people back to me again in English. It was quite confusing at times, but I did my best to keep eye contact with her the whole time she spoke.

Tired and drawn, she sat with her arms around two of her little girls, telling me of her long walks to collect dirty water and the fights that would sometimes break out when water was scarce. Her kids got sick from drinking the water, but she didn't have the money for medical treatment. Through my translator, she begged me, 'Please help us with this water.' I spoke to her through tears, telling her that I also had a little girl (Amelie was three at the time) and couldn't imagine having to do such a thing. I felt bad crying in front of her. I hoped she realised it was empathy.

After we spoke, I joined her on the journey to collect water with the rest of the community, leaving her children behind. I helped her fill her water container but could barely lift it when it was full. The idea that she did this almost every day under the blazing sun was both humbling and distressing.

One of the hardest parts about the trip was having bottles of water wherever we went but being told that we couldn't give them away. As we drove around from place to place, I watched out of the windows as more children from the various communities chased the car down, arms and hands outstretched for whatever we might give them. Of course, I wanted to give away my bottled water, but I was warned not to. Everyone on the team was told the same. If we gave water to one child, there was a risk that they might get picked on or beaten up by other kids, such was the desperation for water in some regions of the country.

The following day, I visited one of the water-points that WaterAid had provided in another community, and it was like another world. Women with bright, smiling faces told me how they only had a short walk to get clean, safe drinking water. I watched as they filled their canisters and did their washing in the sinks, and they told me how much healthier their kids were and how their lives had changed just by having this precious but fundamental need supplied. Although it was at the early stages of the process, I hoped the first village I'd visited would one day have the same facility for clean water as this one, once we'd raised even more awareness with the film we were making.

Throughout these eye-opening and humbling experiences, some of my old worries and fears came bubbling to the surface, particularly my emetophobia, because I wasn't able to wash my hands. I worried when I took a shower and when I ate. It was hard not to feel immensely guilty knowing how privileged I am, and how lucky I was, living the way I did every day.

The people I met were so proud of who they were and where they lived, and their resilience was inspiring to experience. As human beings, we all need a helping hand and a bit of support sometimes to help us thrive, and that's all they were asking for. Nobody wanted everything done for them; they just needed a start. That was the point of my film for the charity, to show how communities can grow and thrive just by having clean water.

The trip to Ethiopia pulled on so many thoughts, feelings and emotions, the main one being the massive sense of responsibility that comes from an experience like that. I went into it wanting to be the best person I could be and do the best job possible. It was such an amazing and humbling thing to have done, and I'm happy to say that since then there have been many more celebrity supporters and high-profile ambassadors for the charity.

Being asked to be a part of Band Aid 20 back in 2004 was another exciting experience. This was a slightly more upbeat version of the iconic Christmas single from 1984, 'Do They Know It's Christmas?' With an incredible line-up of artists that included Dido, Chris Martin of Coldplay, Sugababes, Will Young, Joss Stone, Robbie Williams, Bono – recreating his famous 'tonight thank God it's them' line from the original, and shed loads more. The single ended up becoming the biggest-selling single of 2004, as well as making the Christmas number one. It sold 72,000 copies in the first 24 hours after it was released and stayed at the top of the charts for a total of four weeks, just a week shorter than the original.

I remember the recording day well, although I wasn't hugely present. At that point in my career, I was coming to a crossroads. I felt like everyone else there knew exactly who they were, while I was only just beginning to find out.

Chapter 18

PROJECTS

AS WELL AS the charities, there have also been some interesting TV and stage opportunities in the last ten years, both music-related and otherwise.

In 2013, for *The X Factor*, New Zealand, I flew out to be mentor Melanie Blatt's surprise guest judge on the judges' homes section of the show. It was quite the schedule, however, essentially travelling to New Zealand for 48 hours – what was I thinking? Charl flew over with me, and I think we did the entire trip and recorded the show in the space of about three days. When we arrived, the producers ran me through the agenda for filming, but by then I hardly knew what day it was, I was so jet-lagged.

'We're going to fly you in by helicopter over the archipelago,' one producer told me. 'It'll make for a great shot, and then you'll land at the house and climb out of the chopper in front of the contestants as the surprise guest judge.'

Here we go again, I thought. Small, noisy airborne craft, landing in somebody's garden. Everything I hate crammed into one delicious TV package. Plenty of people would have been thrilled with the experience, but in my case, the surprise for the contestants would be that I survived the journey as much as anything. As usual, I would be professional and push through the fear. It had been a big deal organising everything and leaving Amelie, who was only again still three at the time. If I was going to do it, it might as well be with a spectacular entrance.

Another great job opportunity that came my way was being a judge on the fourth series of *The Voice of Ireland*. One of my initial thoughts was, *Oh, great! I get to be on one of those spinny chairs and press the big red button – fun!* I ended up doing two seasons, working alongside Westlife's Kian Egan, Bressie – a well-known Irish musician – and the gorgeous Una Healy from the Saturdays.

Dublin, one of the greatest cities in the world, became my second home. It was a fun, vibrant place full of warm and friendly people. I loved every visit. At that time, however, I was by then leaving both my girls every weekend, and I really struggled with that. Juggling a career that took me away from home while trying to provide for my family and be a good mum was tricky. Finding the right balance of showing them how much I loved them, but also that Mum has a career was important to me. It continues to be a struggle now.

As for being in Dublin, let's talk about the language barrier with all the local lingo. Being the only Brit, I had to learn fast, but I loved it! Meanwhile, the 'mum' side of me most definitely came out as far as mentoring the contestants went. I tried to give constructive criticism while at the same time passing on some of the things I'd learned throughout my career in a way that was fun and encouraging. I also enjoyed getting to know Una during my time on *The Voice*. Like me, she was a mum with similar responsibilities, so we could share and relate to one another.

While I was filming in Ireland, Nikki came to visit and stay with me a few times. We had many a fun weekend hitting the Irish bar scene and sampling the Guinness. It felt so good to let go and let my hair down – dressing up, bar hopping, drinking cocktails and, as always, laughing a lot.

A few years later, when I agreed to appear as a contestant on *Celebrity MasterChef*, in 2017, there was one thing I hadn't taken into consideration – the fact that I didn't know how to cook. Once again, when the offer to do it came through, I was more interested in the idea of learning a new skill and trying something different. Plus, I'm such a foodie, and love the show, so I thought it would be a good idea.

The truth was, I'd never got into the habit of cooking, and once I left home and got into the band, everything was done for me. It was either catering on the set of the TV shows or on tours, in cafés and restaurants when we were out and about, or, when Jo and I were sharing an apartment together during the filming of the TV series, we might push the boat out and microwave a jacket potato with butter and cheese. That was the extent of our culinary adventurousness!

On the first day of *MasterChef* filming – the mystery box round – where each contestant is given the same ingredients to make a delicious meal – I was faced with beef mince, aubergine, red pepper, mushrooms, ricotta cheese and pasta dough. I recall sort of glazing over when I looked down on it; nothing came to mind immediately, apart from sheer panic. We also had access to a basic larder of spices, tinned kidney beans and tomatoes and a few other essentials to work with. In the end, I was so nervous that I announced to judge Gregg Wallace that I was going for comfort food – 'a shepherd's pie kind of thing'. Gregg kindly pointed out that as it was beef mince, it would be a cottage pie. So that was a good start. Not having enough time to bake the bloody thing, the resulting meal was described as 'Rachel's mince and mash'. So, as you can imagine, I was off to a flying start. Still, the judges liked the taste, and later in the episode, I made pan-fried duck and quinoa, which went down well enough, followed by a triple-chocolate-chip skillet cookie. That was also very good, apart from the fact that I messed up the accompanying banana ice cream so I couldn't serve it. Looking back, the fact that I even did what I did is something to be celebrated. If someone had told me that I'd have put that meal together before walking into that kitchen, I'd never have believed them. In the end, I did OK. I didn't make it into the semi-finals, but it was a great experience and I couldn't believe how far I'd got.

I still don't consider myself to be the most amazing cook, but I get by and we eat healthily. I'm a good 'mum-chef'! I rock a mean spag bol, and I'm great at eating. One of my favourite things to do, and greatest joys, is eating out and trying out new restaurants, usually with a delicious glass of wine in my hand. Japanese, Asian fusion and Italian are probably my favourite cuisines.

In 2019 the stage beckoned, and I toured in the Seventies music review *Rip It Up* along with gymnast Louis Smith, Pussycat Doll Melody Thornton, Lee Ryan of Blue and singer Giovanni Spano. From the start, this sounded like a great job, because I'd be dancing again, which I loved, and how could you not have fun doing a Seventies music show?

Turning up at rehearsals and meeting all the professional dancers was slightly daunting. I wasn't feeling in the best physical shape – it had been a while since I'd done any kind of performing of this kind – and here I was, about to be thrown in at the deep end, trying to learn choreography and music at an incredibly fast pace. Still, I met some gorgeous people, and I got the opportunity to dance with some very talented performers – one of them you might know from *Strictly*: the lovely Kai Widdrington. As a company, we danced and sang our way around the country in suitably sparkling outfits performing big hits from the 1970s, ending up at the London Palladium – an iconic venue for our final shows.

During the run, I had some heartbreaking news. I was on stage, warming up, when I got the call telling me that my Grandma Pearl had passed away, aged 89. She had been unwell for a while, and it worried me being away, but it was such a shock taking that call; I fell to the floor, heartbroken.

Grandma Pearl had always been one of my biggest cheer-leaders, so proud of all I'd achieved. She told me often how much joy my success brought her, and she was the only grandparent I'd been close to growing up. She was the matriarch of the family – tiny, but such a powerhouse, and glamorous to the end, with her leopard-print walking stick and golden-orange hair.

During the show that night, I performed loudly and proudly, singing to the top of the venue, and singing for her. It was my way of getting through the show that night.

After *Rip It Up*, I must have got the bug to perform live again, because in 2020 I decided to throw myself in at the deep end and do a live and intimate cabaret show. Proud Cabaret hosts a colourful, outrageous, burlesque-style extravaganza. A mix of musical comedy, circus and music, featuring everything from burlesque performers and drag queens to aerialists and fire-breathers – all happening while people drink and dine just a few feet from the stage. Proud Embankment in London did a series of shows fronted and hosted by celebrity performers, and I was approached to be one of them for December – right in between Covid lockdowns!

I loved the ambience of the venue, the richness and colour of the place, and the artistry of the people who performed there. It was like stepping into a new world, which is sometimes hard for me in a work sense. Here I was starting something new again, feeling once more a little vulnerable, coming into another new experience. I take so much pride in whatever I take on; I think it's good to be a bit apprehensive because it means you care about what you're doing.

One thing I've learned recently, and always try to keep in mind as an artist, is that whatever I'm doing, I'm bringing 'me' to the table. In the past, I'd struggled with concerns about fitting in to new situations, or not being enough. These days, I know the most important thing is to just be me, and to be fully me. I'm there because somebody wants what I can deliver, and that's enough.

So, with Proud, when doubts and nerves started to creep in, I just reminded myself that I wasn't a performer like them and didn't have to be. I was a performer like *me*!

Being in this wonderfully sultry setting, with faces looking up at you from tables just a few feet away, was a whole new experience, and much more intimate than I was used to. And, as you might imagine, the alcohol in the room was flowing, especially given the season, so as far as audience reaction went, I was never quite sure what I was going to get. What I did know was that they were going to be loud, and that they were probably going to have fun and get involved. This was an audience who'd been stuck indoors. This was an audience who'd been stuck indoors for months on end due to Covid – they were out to enjoy themselves. They were a great crowd to play for – really appreciative and warm.

For my shows, I performed a set of five songs, including 'Sweet Dreams My LA Ex' and 'Some Girls', plus my own rendition of the Christmas classic 'Santa Baby'. During my numbers I was surrounded by some of the stunning female Proud performers and dancers – although I was generally wearing a bit more than they were!

It was a wonderful experience, but it came in the run-up to Christmas 2020 – the Christmas that got cancelled due to Covid – so in the end I only got to do a couple of shows before the venue had to close its doors once more, which was such a disappointment for everyone involved. I would have gone back, but by the time everything was up and running again, I was busy with other commitments.

Chapter 19

EVOLVING

I GOT TOGETHER with my manager Benji Rom in the early days of the pandemic and subsequent lockdowns. He'd worked for my previous management company, InterTalent – headed up by Jonathan Shalit – who I'd been with for a few years after Finch + Partners. I think I'd found the whole management situation tricky back then because I was still unsure of my direction. I was discovering new passions, and the landscape was changing at a fast pace in terms of social media and the online world. It was all catching my attention, and I knew I wanted to somehow get involved.

During my time with InterTalent, I'd often see Benji out and about and at various events as he worked his way up through the team. When he decided to set up his own talent-management company, he approached me asking if I was interested in him representing me, knowing I'd also recently left InterTalent. At that time, I was looking for a smaller, more bespoke management company. I needed something more personal and hands-on than I'd had in the recent past, and Benji's new company, Rom Com Entertainment, felt like it could be a great fit.

When I sat down with him for a coffee one day, I warmed to him straight away, loving his energy and passion. As far as the entertainment industry goes, Benji is one of the good ones.

Some of the things we discussed in those early meetings were my interest in fashion, how the online world was developing, the idea of branding collaborations, and the creative world that I was opening up to online. The entertainment industry is always evolving, and with Covid, everything had flipped and changed again.

Back in the day, at the start of S Club, there was no such thing as social media, so in terms of business it was a new way of working for me, and I wondered where I might fit in with that. I knew I wanted to put my love of fashion into something creative, I just wasn't sure what that would look like or how to structure it.

I enjoyed the creative element of Instagram and the way it could connect you with like-minded people or brands you align with. On the whole, I found it to be a positive and supportive community that I wanted to be a part of. I'd started following lots of influencers, feeling inspired by and enjoying the way they were creating content with various brands. This new inspiration was important because, post my music career and becoming a mum, I'd lost a real sense of self. Fashion had always been a huge part of my

world – having my own sense of style was a way of expressing who I am. Now, I needed to reset and learn how to
make it work for me in a new world and how to turn it
into a business.

Building an online fashion presence felt fun and exciting;
it was something I could be good at and make work while
being a mum. Rebranding myself and building something
new while navigating all the other elements and opportunities within my career was something I welcomed. I found it
challenging and a little daunting at times, but all in the most
positive way. As much as I loved the idea of creating this
wonderful online fashion presence, my tech skills are a work
in constant progress. I'm learning new things every day.

Benji and I were approached by and met with high-street
clothing company Oasis with a view to me working on
some branding. It started off with me creating edits for the
brand – which meant putting together my personal favourites from their line, then styling them my way, which was
great fun. When they did well, the team at Oasis offered me
the chance to collaborate with them on my own line.

This was an exciting project to be involved with, where I
could really get creative and learn more about how the
process worked.

Together, we began with mood boards and ideas, then
we'd look at what was trending and on the catwalks. After
initial thoughts, we took ideas from the mood-board stage
to design, then on to choosing colours and fabrics. I even

got into overseeing the smaller details: buttons, stitching, finessing shapes, adding shoulder pads.

I did four collections for Oasis over two years, and I loved it. They were a great team and I really loved the whole collaborative process. This was a great hands-on learning experience. I sometimes wonder what I would have done had I not been chosen for S Club. Being as driven as I was, perhaps I would have continued on that path and worked my way up in the fashion world.

As well as my passion for fashion, I also loved all things beauty and skincare. As I'm getting older, I'm learning how to feed my skin (and myself) from the inside out, to help with the ageing process. When you've been photographed as much as I have from such a young age, you can be frozen in time in some people's minds. While it's easy to make yourself look really good in a well-posed Instagram shot with the right lighting and make-up, real life is another matter. I understood, as I came into my late thirties and early forties, the insecurities around getting older – especially being in the public eye. I think we all have those insecurities, but at the same time, I'm learning to see the beauty in ageing and growing in every sense.

Chapter 20

CONNECTION

DANCING ON ICE wasn't on my radar at all as far as TV shows went, but I liked ice skating as a young girl. It wasn't something I did for long – but I enjoyed it. So, when Benji called in the summer of 2021 and asked if I'd be interested in taking part in the show the following January, I thought I should at least have a meeting with the producers. Why not? It had come at a time in my life when I welcomed a new challenge and something to get stuck into.

As well as that, I was excited about the prospect of trying something different and learning a new skill, especially after a year or so of restrictions and lockdowns. I didn't really know if I'd be any good at it. I might have ice-skated as a child, but you certainly wouldn't have described it as dancing; this would be a whole new experience. After talking it through with Benji and the show's producers, I decided to go for it.

Leading up to meeting my skating partner for the first time, an American pro-skater called Brendyn Hatfield, I was quite nervous. As soon as I met Brendyn, though – pretty much in that first hour – I connected to his kind, calm and beautiful energy. We've since spoken about this, and he says that he had a similar feeling about meeting me, and, unknowingly, we were both at very similar points in our personal lives. Once the two of us had met and chatted for a while, I knew we were going to get along, and now I was looking forward to doing the show even more.

The training for *Dancing on Ice* was tough, logistically as much as physically, because I had the girls to consider. I tried not to let what was going on in my marriage affect me during the run-up to the show, but it wasn't easy. In some ways, the show gave me a focus, which really helped. Once again, the VT cameras, the interviews, the need to be 'switched on' the whole time, and the knowledge that my every word and facial expression might be captured on film and beamed out to the country, was triggering. On one particular filming day during practice, I was struggling – feeling emotional with everything going on at the time. I was overwhelmed due to the cameras being on me and not getting the routine right. I was stuck in my head, and went into that old familiar protection mode, where I just want to hide. As the cameras rolled, I felt so exposed. In the end, I turned to Brendyn and the camera crew.

'I'm just going to take a break,' I said.

After a breather, I came back on set, and finished my session and my filming, but I went home that night and felt a strong need to share what had happened with Brendyn. In the midst of a high-pressured TV competition with all that was going on in my personal life, I knew there might be a few more moments like the one I'd had that day. Still, this was the first time in a long while that I wanted to – and possibly could – share, open up and allow myself to be vulnerable with someone who I hadn't known very long. It was really scary; I wasn't used to sharing those inner vulnerabilities. This was a real moment of growth for me, and my friendship with Brendyn grew as a result. I knew I could trust him, and as rehearsals continued, our friendship and partnership grew.

As the days went on, I did my best to see *Dancing on Ice* as something fresh and new, and not compare it to past experiences. In the end, however, I realised I struggle with this type of show, even though I enjoy learning from them. Some people are very good at them, but I'm not one of those people.

My experience on the show was a rollercoaster. Once we were off and running, I was all ready to crack on and work hard, building my confidence and skill set on the ice. Brendyn was incredibly patient and such a great teacher, and once we got into the swing of our rehearsal schedule on the ice, I started to learn a few of the basics and even a few tricks, finding my feet. Unfortunately, just a couple of weeks into training with a *Dancing on Ice* coach, before the live shows started, I took a fall and broke my wrist. Straight after the session in which I fell, not realising the damage I'd done, I rushed off to do a shoot with *Hello!* magazine – pushing on with things as I always do. While I was in the chair getting full hair and make-up done for the shoot, my arm was sitting in a bucket of ice – oh, the glamour! Forever the optimist, I convinced myself it was just bruised and would settle down, but no, it got progressively worse as the shoot went on; I even had to have help getting dressed. Eventually, I got through the day and went home. The following day, still in pain, I went for an X-ray to see if I could find out what on earth I'd done to my wrist. In all my forty-five years on this planet, I'd waited until I was doing *Dancing on Ice* to break a bone!

I messaged Brendyn to tell him what had happened, and following that, the producers met. Immediately, there was talk of me potentially not being able to continue the show. I was so gutted that my injury might have signalled the end of the road, but thankfully, I was told I wouldn't have to leave. I did, however, have to keep my arm in a cast, follow strict medical instructions, which meant that I wasn't allowed on the ice for the next six weeks. All this right before the Christmas holidays!

This meant me missing our first scheduled appearance on the show when it began in January. Still, I was determined and committed to making it work. We learned a brand-new routine off-ice in a matter of days, although my confidence had really suffered – then we eventually transferred the routine to the ice.

That wasn't the end of my challenges on the show either. At the end of 2021, we were still getting tested for Covid every Monday. I remember feeling very tired on the day I got tested: groggy, lethargic and headachy. As I get quite a lot of headaches, I didn't really think anything of it. That week, the whole of *Dancing on Ice* was due to attend the ITV Palooza, an annual showcase of the new and upcoming shows on ITV.

On the evening after my Covid test, I met with my stylist at home, who brought an array of gorgeous dresses for me to try on. We also had the alterations lady there, all ready to go once I'd found the right dress. Just as I was getting pulled and pinned in all the right places, the phone rang. It was one of the producers from the show with the news that I had Covid.

I couldn't believe it. I'd just got back on the ice and now I was down to earth with a bump with the news that I'd have to be off again for another ten days. The weird thing was, pretty much immediately after I knew I had it, I started to feel even more unwell. I was a bit scared, too, because at that point I'd never had Covid, so had no idea what to expect.

Thankfully, I only had cold and flu symptoms throughout, but, of course, I had to isolate for the duration of it. All in all, I had missed around six weeks of training, which left me on the back foot. I was starting in a different place to the others, and generally felt a little bit out of it. By the time I finally got to skate on the show, it was incredibly daunting, and my confidence was at an all-time low.

All that considered, I think I was given quite a hard time by the judges. One comment that stood out was that they would have liked to see more confidence and that I didn't give enough, which was really disheartening. Of course, it was a TV show – entertainment and fun for the family – I knew that. Still, when you're invested in something and you're really working hard, putting in the hours, it feels like so much more. Going out for my first show, I suffered the same nerves we all did that first time on the ice, but knowing I'd had so little training, I was particularly insecure and scared. I always feel much more confident when I've prepared, but after all the chaos, I felt the opposite. Given all that, I would have appreciated a slightly softer, more supportive start from the judges. Constructive criticism is one thing, but perhaps they could also have acknowledged how well we'd done considering my injury and the time we'd lost. Despite my nerves, I actually thought we did pretty well, and I'd given it my best.

From a very shaky start, I got to a swift end, with Brendyn and me in the bottom two for both weeks we got to perform. It was a tough competition, too, with some amazing dancers that year. Regan Gascoigne, son of footballer Paul Gascoigne, who ultimately won the show, was fantastic, and ex-Pussycat Doll Kimberly Wyatt was an absolute powerhouse. She was in the final along with Regan and *Strictly*'s Brendan Cole, who was also great.

All in all, I'm still proud of everything we achieved, but in the end I was quite relieved to be voted off. The only thing I was going to miss was Brendyn. With *Dancing on Ice* done and dusted, I thought about him all the time. Although nothing had happened between us, I couldn't get the feelings I was having out of my mind. We'd been on this journey together and built a friendship, but surely that couldn't be the end of it? I wanted to get to know him more and to see him again, but for a while, it didn't seem possible, with my home life as it was. At that point, neither of us had been brave enough to vocalise our feelings for the other, so I couldn't even be sure that he felt the same. It was a confusing and sometimes quite painful time because I had no idea what to do about it. The only people I confided in were Nikki and my therapist. Without them, I honestly don't know what I would have done.

The short solution was WhatsApp. Over the next few weeks, Brendyn and I messaged one another constantly and shared more than we ever did when working together. Not quick 'Hello, how's your day going?' messages, but long, in-depth, emotional messages about what was happening in our lives and how we were dealing with our fractured relationships. From there, we formed an even deeper connection.

I knew I had to tell Brendyn how I felt; it was time for full disclosure. Still, it was a mix of every single emotion because I didn't know if Brendyn's feelings truly mirrored mine. I thought I knew, but this was such a leap of faith for both of us; how could I be sure? All I knew was that I couldn't help the feelings that were developing. There was no stopping it now. I'd never felt this way about anyone, and after all those years of searching, there was no way I was going to let it slip through my fingers.

By the time I was brave enough to tell Brendyn I had these feelings, I'd built it up so much in my head that I thought I might explode. There was still a niggling voice in me telling me he might turn around and say, 'I don't feel the same,' and that voice got louder as the time to confess drew closer. As it turned out, when we eventually met up, I hardly had time to get the words out before he was repeating them back to me. Brendyn had already broken up with his girl-friend, but because Alex and I were still under the same roof, there was a big hurdle yet to overcome.

I knew it wasn't good. I really wasn't happy, but at the same time, it was hard to even think about the reality of breaking up our family and everything that would be lost with that. Alex's family – his mum, dad, sister and her family – had become my family, and his parents were like parents to me. I knew that was going to be a painful separa-tion, too.

In my heart, I knew I would have to make the break at some point, but it felt like jumping off a cliff. It was the hardest decision I've ever had to make. My whole life was entwined with Alex – our history, our children, our home, our families. And as much as I knew it wasn't working, I loved and cared about Alex, and the last thing I wanted to do was hurt him. In the end, I couldn't see any other way forward. We were hurting one another, and our kids in the process, and something had to change.

Around this time, I went to visit my brother at the BMW garage where he worked, as I needed to get my car sorted. While I was there, I spotted a smart Mini Cooper S convertible winking at me from the showroom and thought, *Do you know what? I think it's time for a change! My girls are only little, so they'll fit in that just fine, won't they?*

It was quite unlike me, but I made a spur-of-the-moment decision and ordered it there and then – and I don't regret it. That baby has since taken me on a few fun little trips. Looking back on that day, I see it as an empowering moment when my life was changing direction. It was a reminder that I could make decisions for myself and create my own narrative, which felt wonderful.

Chapter 21

NAVIGATING CHANGE

AFTER THE SHOW finished, Alex and I finally agreed on a trial separation, which was terribly painful. Now, it all felt very real and even more scary. Alex moved into a friend's flat for about a week. There were so many questions, and the fear of knowing we would be hurting our girls if things didn't work out made it even harder. We both knew that if there were hard decisions to come, we'd have to try to minimise the amount of damage that came from those decisions, to protect Amelie and Minnie and keep them feeling as safe as possible.

Eventually after the trial separation the decision was made to separate for good. We were back under the same roof, in the family home, where we could sort everything out and get the house sold, which was incredibly hard for all of us. It was a challenging time. It would have been easier if there had been no love between Alex and me, but that wasn't the case. As with so many things in life, it wasn't simply black or white.

I was scared. I was scared of hurting Alex and the girls. I thought if I hadn't actually said it out loud, it would all be OK, and I wouldn't have done anything wrong.

When Alex and I finally decided to separate for good, our main focus was still our girls. I didn't want them coming out of their childhood with the battle scars I had. The difference was my scars came from someone leaving; with them, I was more worried about what might happen if I stayed. Thinking about everything that had happened to me when my parents' marriage ended, I wanted the opposite for our girls. Where I had the rug pulled from under me with no explanation, discussion or comfort, I wanted to protect them at all costs.

There's really no good way to tell a child that their mum and dad are splitting up, but if there's one thing Alex and I agreed on completely, it was about how we handled situations with the girls. Once we knew that's what was happening, our mission and our goal were to keep our daughters safe.

Speaking to my mum recently about why she never sat me down and told me what was happening with Dad, she says, 'I just wanted to protect you,' and I know that was her way, but ultimately it did the opposite. It left me feeling abandoned and in the dark because no one explained anything, and there was no reassurance from anyone that I was loved and that things would be OK. I was much older than Amelie and Minnie when Dad left, so perhaps I could have helped

Mum if she'd shared. Perhaps we could have been one another's support.

Whatever happened, both Alex and I would always be there for our girls. At the same time, we had to be honest and tell them that Mummy and Daddy couldn't stay together anymore. It was a fine line to walk. Both of the girls are so sharp and knowing, and they'd sensed all was not well for a while. That was one of the hardest things for me leading up to our separation: them knowing things weren't right, but Alex and I not quite having the words to tell them yet.

In the end, when we told them, Amelie went into meltdown. She'd seen it coming, and it was what she feared most. Minnie was much quieter and went into herself, needing to process what she had just heard. Neither of their reactions surprised us, but this was something that had to be done, and we'd done it in the gentlest way we possibly could.

As far as our wider families went, everyone was just trying to navigate their way through it as best they could. Deep down, I think everyone knew we would all come through it and remain close. There was still a lot of love and respect between us all, and time has proved that to be the case.

Being in the public eye, there's always the worry about how other people and the media are going to react to news of a relationship break-up. The day I decided to go public about our separation via social media was more than a little scary. It was only a matter of time before the news got out, so this seemed like the right time to go public and control the narrative. There were people relatively close to us who still didn't really know what was happening because, in some ways, I'd been living a lie. It wasn't because I didn't trust all those people; it was more that I didn't want people talking and word getting out until I had it all straight in my own head.

On the day we announced it, in July 2022, I composed the post and Alex looked it over, making sure he was happy with what we were putting out. Even then, I was full of butterflies. Nikki was with me that night to hold my hand, which was such a huge comfort; I was genuinely scared to press the button. Having always been quite private when it comes to my personal life, releasing something as deeply personal as the breakdown of my marriage into the world was going to take some doing.

'I just wanted to share with you all that after time and consideration the difficult decision has been made for Alex and I to separate. While we are no longer partners in marriage, we will remain partners in parenthood to our beautiful girls and continue with love and respect for each other. *I feel so incredibly grateful for the life we built together and will now continue to be focused on moving forward united as a family.*'

Once it was out there, I was very touched by the amount of love and support that came back to me. People shared their stories with me, some telling me they were going through something similar. It's empowering and lovely when you open up because it allows others to do the same. When you share yourself, others will share, too.

The press picked up on it straight away, which was to be expected, but there wasn't much more to say than what I'd already said in my post. There was no scandal or salacious story; it was simply the sad ending of a relationship.

Writing about it now, I'm remembering one strangely comedic moment during our break-up – let's call it 'vase gate'. We had a lot of vases – who doesn't love a vase? But let me set the scene. We'd finally sold our house – and were preparing for both our moves with the girls – and Alex and I had managed to divide up much of the furniture and things we owned together. Towards the end of that process it got harder, and I think we saw the vases as representing the end.

At one point, our lounge had no furniture left in it and most of our things were in boxes, but we couldn't agree who should get custody of the many vases.

Nikki, who is like family for both of us and was helping us with the move, needed to be Switzerland – the neutral voice – and we took turns, each picking vases, one at a time. It was like a crazy, exhausting whirlwind, packing up our life with Nikki by my side. I honestly don't know what I would have done without her.

Amid all this deliriousness, I came home one night to find a tiny kitten on my doorstep. As I walked in the front door, he was still just sitting there, staring up at me, and I wasn't sure what to do. I had kids, a dog, an Alex, and I was literally about to move out in a week or so.

I certainly wasn't thinking about getting a new cat, but as I started to close the front door, I fell in love with this little ball of fur. I picked him up and brought him inside, and that was it. He'd come to us at my biggest moment of change, and a huge moment of change for the girls. I can't help but think how timely and odd this new little arrival was, and I really do believe he was sent to us.

Of course, I took him to the vet to see if he was chipped, and advertised on local groups, but no one claimed him. The vet said we could adopt him if no one had claimed him in a week – so we did. As I continued with my packing, he stayed right by my side, and the girls affectionately named him Sushi. He brought a little bit of joy into our lives when we needed it most, and I'm grateful to have found him.

As for Brendyn and me, that was something we wanted to figure out in private.

For that reason, our relationship in those early days was very low-key. We didn't go out to dinner or on dates to the cinema together because we knew if we did, we'd have to answer questions we weren't ready for and having just announced the end of my marriage, we didn't feel it was respectful to Alex or to Brendyn's ex-girlfriend to be seen together, while getting to know each other on a deeper level. Now we'd gone from being out and about as friends and professional partners to being in a bubble. While I was still living in our family home, I could only see Brendyn sporadically, so time was precious. There were also a few times when Brendyn had to go back to America, and then the long, deep WhatsApp messages would come back into play. In this new normal, if we weren't talking in person, then we were talking by message. The time apart was hard, but I believe we needed it, because while we were discovering each other, we also needed to discover ourselves.

Chapter 22

BRINGING IT ALL BACK

IN NOVEMBER 2022, all seven members of S Club received a group email from Simon Fuller, reminding us that 2023 would be the twenty-fifth anniversary of the band's formation, and suggesting we should celebrate it with an anniversary tour.

We had reunited once before, in 2015, on our *Bring It All Back* tour, but that was always going to be a short-term thing. The rehearsal period was fairly crazy and intense for me. I was also doing a *Strictly* tour at the time, and I'd not long had Minnie, who wasn't even crawling yet. I don't do things by halves! Looking back on it now, I'm not sure how I managed to make it all work. There was a lot going on, and trying to learn and re-learn S Club dance routines, old and new, while mastering my *Strictly* dances sometimes made my head spin.

The 2015 S Club tour had been a short burst, but a fun reminder of what it meant to be up there performing as S Club. At the end of it, there was a big celebration party in London where the whole team plus all our families and friends got together. It was a great way to end that moment in time before we all went our separate ways. This time, when Simon called, we all agreed that a twenty-fifth anniversary was something worth celebrating. Overall, we were really positive about the idea of another tour, and there was also the idea that maybe this time it could be more than a one-off.

After Simon's call, we started getting in touch with one another regularly again, via emails and WhatsApp. I was relieved to be hearing from Jon again. He'd been off-grid for a while – uncontactable and offline – so I'd been worried about him. I knew he'd gone to live in India for a while, but not much else, so it was wonderful to hear his voice and see his messages.

Before long, we were in discussions about what a 2023 S Club tour might look like. Our WhatsApp group was buzzing with ideas, and there was a lot of excitement around the prospect of it. Again, there was a noticeably different energy surrounding us reforming this time around, and talk of other things happening after the tour – a reigniting of us as a band rather than it being a short-lived nostalgia trip. Now, we were all older with more life experience, and all, I think, in a different headspace; ready to commit to something more long term.

I couldn't have imagined then how drastically things were going to change before we set foot on stage for our first show. None of us could.

During the early part of 2023, we did a few things as a seven-piece. One of them was appearing in a sketch for Comic Relief, where we were supposed to be auditioning to represent the UK in the Eurovision Song Contest in front of a panel that consisted of Lulu, Graham Norton and Sam Ryder, who'd come second in the contest for the UK the previous year. From there, the seven of us had a few meetings to talk things through and there was so much excitement and a real buzz surrounding us coming back together as a band. In fact, when the tickets went on sale, some venues sold out within minutes, and we found ourselves adding extra shows to accommodate the demand.

I sometimes underestimate how things affect me when there's a lot going on. After the big announcement of our tour, we were invited to the BRITs early in 2023. At the time, I'd just got divorced, recently moved out of my house and into a flat with the girls, and we were in the midst of the S Club reunion. There was a lot happening but I just kept pushing through it, without really taking a breath or giving myself time to ease into what was my new normal. In short, I was exhausted.

On the morning of the BRITs I felt fine, but as the day wore on things changed. It wasn't anything too bad at first – an uncomfortable feeling and a bit of a headache, which I put down to anxiety. I know what to do when I feel that way – eat properly, stay relaxed and generally look after myself. As the evening went on, it got worse, and so did my headache. I've suffered this kind of thing a few times before, although not for some time, and it becomes quite debilitating. It sometimes gets to the point where I can barely hold a conversation.

When the time came, I had fun on the red carpet at the Royal Albert Hall with Tina and Jo. We did the interviews we needed to do, and had a great time chatting with everyone. By the time I sat down at my table, ready for the show to start, I felt considerably worse; my head was banging and I couldn't breathe properly. Jo had gone home by then, so I was sitting next to Tina at a table full of Universal Music executives and team members – the label S Club had recently re-signed with. I tried my best to push it aside and join in, chatting with everyone, but in the end, it was hopeless. I told Benji I couldn't stay for the awards, and that I needed to get out of there as soon as possible. I didn't see a second of the show.

Once outside the venue, I got into the car that was taking me home, sweating and feeling nauseated. As we drove through London towards home, I undid my dress, hoping it might ease my breathing.

When I finally reached home, I got undressed and crawled into bed, but by then, I was in the grip of a full-blown panic attack. The girls were staying with Alex that night, so I was completely on my own, and as anyone who's suffered a panic attack will tell you, it can be bloody terrifying.

Thank God for Nikki, who drove straight over and got

into bed with me. She just sat with me while we watched the BRITs. I'd been so excited to watch it in real life, but as I slowly started to calm down, I realised that what I needed in that moment, after a life-changing few years, was my PJs and the telly on with Nikki by my side. Thankfully, when I woke up the following morning, I felt much better.

I don't experience panic attacks that often these days, although I did again a few months later on the video shoot for our single 'These Are the Days'. I had the same feeling of not being able to breathe, but thankfully I managed to suppress it for most of that day so nobody would have known. I got through it that time, but at 11pm, once we'd finished the shoot, I was practically hanging out of the car window on the way home.

It's hard to know why I suffer with this kind of thing. I recently saw a doctor about this and the debilitating headaches I get every month. We talked about issues around hormones during perimenopause, but she thinks my problems are a mix of that and anxiety-triggered feelings. I'm now doing everything I can to keep my hormones and my body well balanced. The anxiety part is something I'm still working on.

In April 2023, I received a call that would change everything; it was from Gayla, who'd been one of our most trusted members of the 19 Management team from the early days of S Club. She'd since left the company, but she was on board to help us organise and put together the new tour.

That day, she called me for an update on how everything was going, and expressed concern about Paul.

'I'm a bit worried. I've been calling him for the last day or so, but I can't get hold of him,' she said. 'I've messaged him, but he hasn't responded, which is unlike him; he's usually the first one to get back to me.'

Gayla could see that he hadn't even read her WhatsApp messages – no blue ticks – which worried her even more, and, in turn, worried me. Yes, he could have lost his phone, but surely he would have found a way to let everyone know if that had been the case?

'Well, how long has it been?' I asked.

'It's been a few days,' Gayla said. 'I'm quite worried.'

My head immediately went to an uneasy place, I don't know why, but I then tried to reassure myself it would all be fine.

'OK, well, we'll all message him and try to get in contact,' I said. 'It's probably nothing.'

Only a couple of days before that Paul had organised a Zoom call with all of us, just for a catch-up. It wasn't something I normally would have expected Paul to do, but he'd seemed in great spirits and was really looking forward to getting things moving. I remember thinking how lovely it was that he had reached out to everyone in that way.

Deep down, though, I didn't believe it was nothing, and after I'd messaged him myself to no avail, I was even more concerned. Paul had been so excited and optimistic about the tour, so up for it; if he wasn't answering messages to Gayla and the rest of us, something was clearly wrong.

At 9.30 the following evening, 6 April, we were all asked to join a group phone call. It was a call I'll never forget. Gayla told us that she'd managed to find Paul's brother on Instagram and told him of her concerns, especially with Paul living on his own. That had led to the dreadful discovery of what had happened. When Gayla said those terrible words, that Paul had passed, I took in the biggest, loudest gasp of breath. My girls were in bed, but my reaction woke them up, and they both came running in, clearly worried about me. I tried to pacify them and get them to go back to bed, while everyone was still on the phone, all trying to process the tragic news. I ended up having to leave the call for a while so I could settle the girls, reassuring them that I, and everyone they loved, was OK, and that I would speak to them in the morning.

During the rest of the call, everyone was in utter shock. There were moments of silence, disbelief and tears, but we all just stayed on the phone together, our hearts broken.

Over the next few days, Paul never left my thoughts. It had been a wonderful and enlightening experience for me to get to know the man that Paul had become in the months leading up to his passing. He was such a gorgeous and sensitive soul, but troubled in some ways. I don't want to go deeply into someone else's personal story; that doesn't seem right. Suffice it to say that, like all of us, he had struggles and was finding his way.

Now, having taken in the awful news and sat with it, we knew there were decisions to be made on a way forward. Initially we just needed time, to process and grieve. I realised how monumental it was, and, like everyone, I was devastated, but there was never a moment when we thought the tour wouldn't happen. In my mind, and the bands', the fact that Paul had passed away meant that now, more than ever, we had to do it – for him and for us. We just needed time.

In early May, we put out a video on our socials explaining to fans that we'd been taking time to remember our beloved Paul and to say that the tour would still be going ahead, albeit without Hannah, who'd decided she no longer wanted to be a part of it.

From then on, the tour took a new direction. We changed the name of it to *The Good Times* tour, after a song from our 2001 album *Sunshine*, on which Paul sang the lead vocal. We wanted to keep Paul in mind and make the show a celebration of him – for him to be a part of it still.

We also recorded new music, putting out a single for the first time in twenty years. 'These Are the Days' was a song that had been around for a long time. It had been written by our long-time musical director and his wife, Johanne, a few years before, and when the subject of us releasing new music came up, particularly after Paul's passing, the sentiment and lyrics really seemed to suit where we were at. Once it was decided that this would be the song for us to record as a single, songwriter Cathy Dennis did a bit of re-working of the lyrics, and we were good to go. The lyrics were beautifully nostalgic; a nod to S Club back in the day and, in many ways, paying tribute to Paul. It was about where we'd come from, where we were, and how we might move forward. On the day we recorded it, we knew it was the perfect song for that moment in time. It was great working with Simon Ellis and Cathy Dennis again, and a lovely way to remember Paul and everything we'd been through together.

Chapter 23

S CLUB PARTY

OVER THE YEARS, one of the many positive things about S Club was that we all got on. Unlike some bands you'd hear about, there were no major bust-ups or fights. I remained close to Jo and Jon throughout; Brad was like a brother to me. I wasn't as close with Paul as I was with some of the others back in the day, but interestingly, when the band first got back together, we had some good in-depth chats. I always loved Paul, but I feel like if he'd been with us now, I'd have got closer to him than when we were younger. As an adult, I saw him in a very different light; noticing a deeper, more thoughtful side to him. When I was younger, I think I missed some of those qualities, but Paul and Hannah were very close – they always gravitated to one another. Tina and I also weren't as close back in the day, but that's no longer the case. Getting to know her on a deeper level as grown-ups and as parents, and swapping mum stories, has been wonderful.

After Paul died, we had a few sessions with a therapist – as a band. It was something our management suggested, and we all discussed it, deciding it was a good way forward. It turned out to be incredibly helpful. We're all very different people who'd all gone our own ways after the band split. The therapy, I think, supported us in respecting, accepting and embracing our differences, as well as helping us to deal with such a huge loss as a group. As young people in S Club 7, we never really discussed emotions, feelings or anything deeply personal, at least not as a group. Because Paul had passed away not long after we'd all come back together, those sessions helped us to talk to one another about his death, to be honest about how we all felt, and then learn to deal with those feelings, both separately and collectively.

As full rehearsals began, our closeness grew, but there was quite a lot of raw emotion from the loss of Paul. As things went on, the tour started to feel more about honouring and celebrating him. At times, it was like he was there with us, as we kept finding new ways and new moments where we could bring him into the show.

Despite Paul and Hannah not being there, there was still a lot of joy during rehearsals. It's funny how I could hardly remember any of the routines, while Jo, on the other hand, knew every step and move. Still, it was fun and interesting learning it all with a talented new choreographer, all reconnecting at a different time of our life and having fun. The close bond we all had resurfaced, as did all the old in-jokes we'd shared over the years. There's such a special chemistry when we're together, and there's magic in our differences.

There were also some overwhelming moments. I was moving home for the third time in a year, and it was all very last minute. In fact, I was actually moving in the week before we went on tour, and, true to form, I was often quite hard on myself, feeling like I should know every step in the show the second I'd been shown it. I always expect to know it all straight away, and when I don't, I can get frustrated. Knowing that about myself and being more self-aware these days, I was able to step away from that and give myself a break.

Thank goodness we had such an amazing choreographer, and that we learned the show in order, which I was very grateful for. We had such a great team around us, which felt like family from the beginning. My S Clubbers, the gorgeous team at Simon's rebranded company, XIX, plus Nikki, Benji and Cindy, were all involved, as well as Nicky our incredible choreographer, our glam squad Malin and Amy, Maddie in wardrobe, our brilliant tour manager Mark and even our little minis, who would visit to dance along with us. It was a family feeling and we all looked after each other.

The technical rehearsal was in a huge production facility. It was very exciting walking into that massive space, watching the stage come to life, and seeing the video screens and production evolve. We'd watched it all build layer by layer, from our first dance rehearsal in an East London dance studio to this.

Our tour bus was amazing, with four lounges, a kitchen, and beds for all of us. The idea was for us to sleep on it for the duration of the tour, but after two nights of that, all of us girls had a different take on the sleeping arrangements. As promised, we'd given it a go, but now it was a case of, *No, let's not do this anymore.* The truth is, we aren't girls anymore; we're women, and we wanted the privacy of our showers and bathroom facilities, not to mention a proper bed to sleep in after doing a full-on show.

With age and with life experience, it felt good to be able to ask for what we wanted or needed to feel comfortable. It was a very different world to the early days of the band, when I was always so afraid to speak up about things that were important to me. But I'd worked so hard on myself over time, and I had this new strength to show for it.

Not living on the tour bus turned out to be a lovely thing because us girls would end up going back to a hotel and having a glass of wine together after a show. Meanwhile, the boys stayed on 'the party bus', which suited them. They loved hanging out and partying with our crew, who were a great bunch of people with a really good energy among them.

Another good reason to be away from the bus was that everyone got ill. Jon and Tina both got sick and people were losing their voices. I was lucky; at that point I'd managed to avoid it. Still, everyone who got sick were absolute troopers and pushed through. We had to!

Leading up to the first night in Manchester, I was all over the place. I always got very nervous before live appearances, and I was worried about how I would cope with those nerves now. Would I still have the resilience of youth; would I just power through? Before every show we would get our call, go to get our mic packs on, and have a moment together as a band to get the party started. As soon as that music kicked in, I got the buzz. Then, walking out as the doors opened and looking over a sea of people was just wonderful. As soon as I'm out there performing, everything else falls away, and it's like I'm flying. I love connecting with an audience, seeing their faces, seeing them smiling and waving back at me. It's a very special feeling. For most of the people in the audience, S Club had been part of their childhood and growing up, so that mix of love, nostalgia and excitement was a strong one. Added to that was the fact that although Paul was gone, he was very much present in our show, and there was so much love in the room. There were so many emotions in play, for the fans and for us. It's not something you often see in a pop show.

Playing in London is always special. Aside from it being home, we know there's going to be family, friends, as well as our management and record company teams, all there to watch, support and celebrate with us.

The first O2 date was overwhelming to say the least. The day started off with a fresh set of eyelashes and new hair extensions, so I needed to be at the venue extra early after travelling down from Birmingham the night before (the things we do in the name of beauty!). From then on it was back-to-back press interviews and TV cameras, plus I recorded a Heart Radio show from backstage. I also had a photographer there to capture some of the magic backstage moments with my family and friends, as well as some on-stage action. This was the first time the girls had come to see me perform live on stage as part of S Club, so it was a pretty big deal for them, too.

All day, I felt a rush of adrenaline, nerves and energy, and it got stronger in the build-up to the show. This was a new chapter in my life, and to be able to share this part of me with everyone I love meant so much. I'll never forget playing the O2 on *The Good Times* tour. It's an incredible venue, and when I stepped out and saw the sea of people, all on their feet ready to party with us for the next few hours, I felt such a buzz.

After the show, 19 Management threw a party. It was lovely to see Simon Fuller again after all those years, reconnecting and celebrating something that was so special to all of us, reliving memories that had been so much a part of all our lives.

Day two at the O2 was equally special, although slightly calmer, with not as much to squeeze into the schedule. That day, I could simply get show-ready, then get out there to perform for our fabulous S Club fans.

During the matinee show that day, we all brought our kids on stage during 'Reach'. It was a moment I will always treasure, and with everyone involved in the production having the best time together, it really did feel like a massive family event.

That day also symbolised how far Alex and I had come in navigating our co-parenting, as he was there with his new partner, his parents and our girls. For us, it was a moment of coming together, supporting one another and becoming a blended family.

My mum was also swept up in the moment. I speak to her on most days, even if it's just a check-in and quick hello. Two days after the London show, though, she called me still buzzing, telling me how proud of me she was. It made her so happy, her reliving the joy of watching us perform and reminding herself what S Club had brought into her life. It felt good knowing that Mum had got so much from the reunion, and that she could express it in that way to me.

A while before that, I'd had a conversation with her where she acknowledged not being there for us when we were younger.

'I wasn't around much after Dad left, was I?'

It was like she was saying she was sorry without actually saying it. She was feeling and acknowledging it and, I think, hoping that I would say, 'I understand and it's OK.'

But I found it hard to do that.

What I do understand now is how difficult it was for her at that time, and I guess that's the difference. I've always been interested in psychology and why people behave the way they do. Lately, Mum has been trying to talk more about our childhood. She's talked about my dad and how she saw things, and although I'm happy that she's opening up a bit, I'm aware it's not always easy for her. I appreciate Mum reaching out to start these conversations, and I'm learning how to connect with her with an open heart and compassion.

I believe Mum was, in her way, trying to protect my brothers and me from certain events. Again, I can see now the human flaws in play. It doesn't make all the hurt and pain go away, but it at least brings understanding and compassion on my part.

Going through my own separation with children, I understand more than ever the challenges my mum had to face on her own, and I appreciate everything she went through. I just wish she had let me in.

* * *

As on any big music tour, there had to be a bit of drama. The second night of the tour had been postponed due to a power outage at the Bank Arena Liverpool. Because of this, we tagged on a rescheduled date at the end of the tour. We were all happy to be giving the ticketholders who'd missed out on a chance to see the show, but this second attempt was even more of a disaster.

In the middle of performing 'Alive', which was three songs from the end of the show – just before 'Reach' and the encore, 'Never Had a Dream Come True' – everything shut down. And I mean everything: lights, sound, music, video screens. It was a complete blackout. One minute we were in a world of colour and energy, and the next it was a void of nothingness.

In the darkness, sirens started going off, and Jon and I swapped glances. The next thing I knew it was a 'code red' and the building had to be evacuated. Meanwhile, we were all still on stage, not knowing what the hell we were supposed to do or which way to go. The next ten minutes were chaos, as we tried to find our way back to our dressing room. Jon was my hero, grabbing my hand and leading me off stage, not realising poor Jo had been stuck on the top of the stage on her own when all the power went off. We can laugh about it now!

When the dust settled, we all ended up in one of the dressing rooms, while people fed us information as it came. It turned out to be exactly the same power failure problem that had forced us to cancel on our second night, only this time the outage had set off the building's alarms. I remembered hearing one audience member saying, 'Oh, not again,' as everything went off, but in my panic, I hadn't made the connection with what had happened previously. By the time I realised it was a false alarm, I'd taken my mic pack off and was gripping a large glass of wine in a shaky hand. Then someone came in and said they wanted us to finish the show if we were happy to do so. Members of the audience who'd been evacuated came back into the arena, and we went on and started 'Alive' again, as we all wanted to make sure we finished the show. The fans deserved it, so we made sure we ended on a huge high.

One of my favourite things about the tour was meeting fans at our meet-and-greet, which was so lovely and, at times, moving. We were meeting grown mums and dads who we'd met when they were kids themselves. The reaction of some of them as they saw us was incredible. Some were crying; others told us how we'd got them through tough times in their young lives.

One woman, dressed up to nines, told us, 'I'm wearing this because of you. You allowed me to be myself and express who I am.'

Another told us how she was bullied at school but would come home and watch our show and feel so much joy through the music. It's incredible how those childhood experiences and memories were still engrained in many of those thirty- or forty-something people. I guess most of us are nostalgic for the best bits of our childhood, and in coming to our show, our audiences were immersing themselves in something that helped them recapture some of that. Many of them brought their kids with them – a whole new generation of S Clubbers.

One particular moment at a meet-and-greet got to all of us. An older couple came with a picture of their little girl with all seven of us – back in the day. She'd met us through the Make-A-Wish foundation, and her parents told us that five months after the photo was taken, their little girl had passed away. Now, they'd come to see our show again, all these years later, in memory of her. We were all in tears as they told us their story.

As an artist, when you're just doing your job, it's easy to forget what an impact you can have on someone's life. You care about the work, and you try to make it the best that it can be, but it can mean so much more to people than loving your music or singing along to a song on the radio. I never imagined how much it might mean to our fans to see us together again until it actually happened.

What really shone through was the diversity within our fans – young, old, straight, gay, trans and of all races. That was always what S Club was about – being whoever you are or want to be. That's what our world was and is – joy, love, colour, kindness. It might sound cheesy, but I think it's what we need right now. For me and many others, our *Good Times* tour came at the perfect time. It was a couple of hours of happiness.

Chapter 24

FINDING ME

I ADMIRE SO many women in the public eye. One of my absolute favourite pop artists is Kylie Minogue. She has always been my pop icon, right since childhood. For me, Kylie was the one: a bright, creative woman who has always sought out cool, interesting ways of expressing who she is. She started out as a pop princess from the Stock Aitken Waterman stable, delivering great pop hits that were written for her, but over thirty-odd years she has gone on to be a respected songwriter and recording artist. If I think pop star, I think Kylie!

There are also many other great women out there who know exactly what to do with the voice they have. That's something I feel passionate about and would like to do more of. I have this platform to do something amazing, and I want to make a difference and do positive things with my voice. I realise now that I've already done that in lots of ways, but I'm looking forward to doing more. It's one of the reasons I wanted to write this book. Not simply to tell my life story but to perhaps empower other young women who struggle with any of the things I may have struggled with.

We're all guilty of comparing ourselves to others, and sometimes we have this perception that people in the public eye have it all sussed. If only that were the case. I watched the Robbie Williams documentary recently, and it really resonated with me. Seeing his struggles play out made me realise that everyone has different ways of dealing with their demons. Robbie's was to go all out – everything to excess. Mine was the total opposite – to exert as much control as possible, to the point where I was holding myself back in lots of ways.

I hope by being honest about the struggles I've had it might resonate with people who recognise some of those things within themselves. I'm now learning that when I'm authentically myself, that's enough, and that feels empowering.

I think it's important to open up conversations and share ourselves. I want to shout out loud about giving validation to young people. I believe sometimes kids suffer with anxiety and depression because they don't yet know how to express their fears and concerns, or they feel misunderstood or not heard. They turn it all inwards, and the result is anxiety of some form. Self-expression is a huge part of a child's mental wellbeing, and I still don't think we put enough importance on that.

* * *

Like me, my daughter Amelie has struggles with worry and anxiety. She's an incredibly deep thinker with a wonderfully active imagination, but interestingly, she's inherited some of the phobias I grew up experiencing – in particular emetophobia. Knowing how to help and offer her the tools she needs to combat it has been challenging, because in many ways I'm still trying to find them myself. We all know that kids are often like little sponges, and sometimes I think they're more emotionally intelligent than we are as grown-ups – they just don't have the understanding or maturity yet to articulate it.

Unknowingly, sometimes our kids become a mirror of ourselves and we learn so much from them. I've been on an incredible learning journey through my girls and we're building such a wonderful support network for them, but especially to help Amelie navigate her struggles; it takes a small army. If I'm truly honest, Amelie's struggles have been really painful at times. And now as a parent I have a greater understanding of why my parents didn't know how to give me what I needed in my life. If a child grows up in a home with parents who aren't emotionally mature, it can be very damaging and really affect a child's self-worth. It's not about blame, it's about learning and growth.

* * *

In the summer of 2023, once Amelie, Minnie and I were settled in our new place, I decided to take them away on holiday. I had mixed emotions about the trip, and at one point I even questioned whether I was making the right decision. This was my first solo trip as a parent with the girls, and I was nervous and worried about the 'unknown' of it all. But it was part of our new start and of a healing process after the separation.

We went to the beautiful island of Majorca, which I'd decided was a perfect destination – not too far, and some-where we could feel safe and relaxed.

We had such an incredible time. I had quite a few reflec-tive moments on my sunbed, watching all the families enjoying time away together, and dads playing in the pool with their kids. There was an odd mix of loneliness and joy in watching my girls play, being away with them, and feel-ing proud of myself for taking that step.

A day or so into the trip, we met a lovely blended family, who also had two girls that Amelie and Minnie made friends with. It felt special for me, connecting with this couple, who were a wonderful example to me of how relationships and blended families can work.

I went through so many different emotions during our holiday, but overall it was very empowering. This was a new normal for me, so I guess it was something I needed to feel and go through to get to the other side. If anything, it just reminded me that we need to do the things that scare us, that push us out of our comfort zones, because the growth that can come from that is invaluable.

I'm very proud of how Alex and I have come through our break-up. There have been some incredibly rocky moments, for sure, and I'm not under any illusions that there won't be more challenges while we are learning to parent in a new way.

As far as the separation goes, I feel like Minnie and Amelie have also grown through all of this. It's made them more resilient, although I'm constantly checking in with them. I've tried not to shield them to the point where they don't know what's happening, and to protect them but be open and honest – that's my approach.

As people, we often live at 100 miles per hour – I certainly do – and like everyone, I make mistakes and sometimes get it wrong, and that's OK. When you see it happen, all you can do is acknowledge it and then help one another heal, recover and move forward.

Now that things between Alex and me are in a better place, instead of seeing us fight, the girls see us working on treating one another with kindness and respect. On Amelie's thirteenth birthday in November, we all went to the Wolseley for dinner – Alex and his parents, my mum and Russell, Amelie, Minnie and me – and it was so special. We've come through a patch that was extremely difficult, but our goal was always to make sure that the girls felt loved and that their mum and dad were communicating, and that's what we are both striving for.

Christmas Eve we all went for a wonderful blended family dinner, and Christmas morning Alex and his new partner came to open presents with us all in our festive PJs. This and moments like it only cement what a great dad Alex is, and I'm grateful he is always going to be there for them.

In past relationships and my career, I've sometimes gone along with certain people or ideas in the hope that they will eventually lead me to what I'm searching for. When my dad left and my relationship with him started to fall apart, it broke my heart and made me question my belief system. How could a love that I'd trusted in so much, and that meant so much to me, be gone? How could my dad not love me anymore? It hurt deeply, and, subconsciously, I put up every barrier possible to stop that hurt from ever happening again. Add to that the layer of fame from a young age and my mistrust of some people's motives, and it was as if I'd built my own castle.

Love and connection became unfamiliar to me. Throughout my life, I've struggled to allow myself to go there because I'm so terrified it will be taken away. One of my first loves of my life was my dad, and when I lost that love it devastated me. Trying to make sense of that loss stayed with me throughout my adult life.

* * *

I'm happy to say that things with my dad are so much better now, with special thanks to a few too many points on my driving licence. Yes, if getting divorced, moving house three times, starting a tour and parenting my girls wasn't enough to keep me busy, I thought I'd throw a driving ban into the mix. There's no exciting story to tell, and it was all very frustrating, but I'm happy to say that something positive came from it.

My ban came not long before the Christmas break, the time when we're all rushing around in preparation, and getting together with family and friends. Wanting to make the best of a bad situation, and knowing my dad was between jobs and wanted to keep busy, I decided to ask him if he fancied helping me out.

When he said yes it felt like a real connecting moment, both knowing that we would be spending time together, and getting to know one another again.

Now, when I work out my schedule, I book my dad in, and our trips together have been enlightening and a lot of fun. We laugh, we catch up, we have a bit of carpool karaoke, and generally enjoy each other's company. We're both very different people to when we last spent this much time together, and I'm grateful for that; grateful to have the opportunity to grow and move on. I'm finding out new things about my dad all the time, and in turn I'm sharing my thoughts and experiences with him.

One thing that hasn't changed is our love of music. We

play all the greats, singing the music he first introduced me to when I was a little girl and reminiscing.

I'm also experiencing a reconnection and beautiful new relationship with my mum. I'm excited to explore our growing bond. I value her and everything she has done for me, as I do my brothers Jason and Leigh, who I love dearly. Now I feel comfortable being me and letting the people I love in, knowing my boundaries. I feel safe knowing I can be open, and I can allow myself to love and be loved without the fear I was carrying in the past.

Over the past few years, I've been on an extensive self-help journey. For so long, I've had questions about why I found it challenging to connect deeply in relationships, why I was never fully able to be myself, and why I so often lived in my head, overthinking everything. Therapy has been good for me. I sometimes think everyone should do it! The woman that I've been seeing for a long time has become more than a therapist; she's something of a life coach too. Like a wise, wonderful and warm aunt, she's someone I can talk to about anything, and she gives me advice when I really need the guidance. Often a good therapist doesn't even say very much, they just allow you the space to figure stuff out on your own. With me, there were no giant, explosive epiphanies, just a slow journey of self-discovery. It's been like a puzzle where you gradually find the piece and eventually think, *Oh, yeah! That goes there.*

My journey through all this is a long one – slow and steady. I'm taking it in baby steps. What I've realised is that you can love and be loved in so many different ways. I know it's a cliché, but you really do have to love yourself first before you can give love and be loved fully. I'm also learning to ask for what I need in my relationships. I'm learning to have stronger boundaries and to know what I want in my life and my relationships, and what I deserve. I believe that if we are open to learning and growing, we will find our way.

Now I appreciate relationships in a different way. Yes, they can be complicated, but I can see how beautiful they are when they're real. I'm excited to continue nurturing all the relationships I have in my life. The fact that I can say all that out loud now is quite something.

Recently, Brendyn and I decided to move in together. It feels like a fresh start, and we're enjoying making a home. We both knew how much we loved and cared about each other, so this next step felt right, and we're excited for this new chapter. Even so, it was a slow and well-thought-out process to get to this next step. In the lead-up to the change, I wanted the girls to get to know Brendyn well and be comfortable with the idea. Now, watching their relationship grow adds another layer of joy to my life and it fills my heart.

Reflecting back on all this, and on my life, I'd like to think I'm someone who is striving to live in the moment, and always tries my best to be present. Experience has taught me to trust in the process, and to listen to myself more. It's exciting to find myself in a place, now, where I'm allowing myself to feel however I feel and know that's OK.

I'm learning to sit in the discomfort of certain situations and not always be in control. I want to keep growing; striving to be the best version of myself that I can be.

There are so many goals and projects I'm dreaming big for – seeing the world and making memories. I feel lucky to have had the experience and opportunities I've had throughout my career, and the chances to learn on the job. But there's always more, and that excites me!

It suddenly hit me, after I recently recorded a show for Heart Radio, how incredibly varied my career has been – from music and performing in front of huge audiences, to acting in movies and TV shows, supporting charities, presenting and fronting documentaries across the globe, and even dipping my toes into the world of fashion. And now I'm writing a book! It's quite the CV, and I'm so grateful for all of it.

Now, I'm looking forward to life's next adventures, knowing that whatever happens, I am enough and I deserve to be heard. We all do!

ACKNOWLEDGEMENTS

I WANT TO start by saying a huge thank you to Nikki for all your time, love, encouragement and endless support. You've been incredible. Thank you for always being by my side and being my biggest cheerleader.

Benji, for all your passion, care and hard work.

Darling Brendyn, thank you for all your love and support, for giving me all the space and time I needed throughout this process and for always being there for me.

Amelie and Minnie, I'm so grateful to be your mummy. Thank you for driving me to be the best version of myself. You girls are my world and I love you with all my heart.

Terry, for all your guidance, patience, care and support – I think we need that glass of wine now!

Lastly, to Imogen and everyone at HarperCollins. Thank you for the opportunity to share my story and for making this book possible.

PICTURE CREDITS

All photographs are courtesy of the author, with the following exceptions:

Section 1
Plate 6: (top) Linda Stone

Section 2
Plate 1: (top) Ken McKay/Shutterstock; (bottom) Dave Hogan/Distributed by Getty Images on behalf of the Band Aid Charitable Trust
Plate 2: (bottom left) PA Images/Alamy Stock Photo
Plate 3: (top left) Guy Levy/BBC; (bottom left) Sean McMenomy

Plate 4: (top) Nikki Glazer; (bottom left) Sasha Benjamin Photography; (bottom right) Rom Com Entertainment

Plate 5: (bottom) Matt Frost/ITV/Shutterstock

Plate 6: (top left) Matt Frost/ITV/Shutterstock; (top right) Nikki Glazer; (bottom) Heart Studio for Rachel Stevens 'This is Heart 00s'/Matt Crossick/Global

Plate 7: (top left) David Fisher/Shutterstock; (top right and bottom) Sasha Benjamin Photography

Plate 8: (top left) Nikki Glazer; (bottom left) Bernie Karkar; (top and bottom right) Sasha Benjamin Photography